Touch All the Bases

The Culture and Idioms of
America's Pastime — Baseball

by Jolinda Osborne

Touch All the Bases: The Culture and Idioms of America's Pastime – Baseball Stories for Learning Useful Business Idioms, Volume 3

© 2011, 2005, Intercultural Communication Services, Inc.

All rights reserved. No portion of this book may be reproduced in any form or by any means without written permission from the copyright holder and publisher. The scanning, uploading and distribution of this book or accompanying audio program via the Internet or via any other means without the permission of the publisher is illegal and punishable by law.

This is a work of fiction. Names, characters, organizations, and incidents are the product of the author's imagination or are used fictitiously. Any resemblance to actual persons living or dead is entirely coincidental.

Audio recording of downloadable story by Rob Metcalf Studio
All illustrations and music used by permission
Cover design: Barrentine Design
Take Me out to the Ball Game sung by Charbonneau Spring Ridge Golden Oldies

Published by Intercultural Communication Services, Inc., Portland, Oregon, U.S.A. Intercultural Communication Services, Inc. publishes quality educational books and video products for non-native English speaking professionals.

ISBN: 978-1461157182

Library of Congress Catalogue Number: 2011930236

For more information about other volumes in the *Stories for Learning Useful Business Idioms Series*, to learn about other educational products, or to enquire about bulk orders, please visit *Jolinda Osborne Intercultural Communications* at www.jolindaosborne.com

Contents

Introduction	Page 5
How to Get the Most from this Book	Page 7
Story	
First Inning	Page 9
Second Inning	Page 17
Third Inning	Page 21
Fourth Inning	Page 29
Fifth Inning	Page 37
Sixth Inning	Page 39
Seventh Inning	Page 46
Eighth Inning	Page 50
Top of the Ninth Inning	Page 57
Bottom of the Ninth Inning	Page 63
Baseball Fundamentals	Page 68
Resources for Continued Learning	Page 70
Index of Idioms and Cultural Vocabulary	Page 72

Introduction

One of the best ways to learn idioms is to understand the cultural context from which they arise. This book, as well as other books in the **Stories for Learning Useful Business Idioms** series, teaches you many commonly-used idioms and expressions heard in business. It also expands your cultural awareness by presenting the idioms in stories set in America.

Idiomatic expressions give speech its color and vitality, and they convey subtle meaning in ways not possible through formal language. Idioms are groups of words that, joined together, differ in meaning from the literal meaning of each separate word. As a student of English, you will find that your speech sounds more natural and you connect with people in a deeper way if you incorporate more of these idioms into your conversations.

Idioms sometimes originate from slang — the informal phrases and newly-coined expressions that people, especially young people, spontaneously create. Slang that becomes widely used by everyone in the culture may be accepted into the dictionary. But more often, idioms arise over the centuries out of activities specific to a culture: their transport [sailing, cars], means of livelihood [fishing, farming], field of study [medicine], universal human experiences [war, love], the arts [music], and even a culture's food and leisure activities.

One of the richest sources of American idioms is sports, especially baseball. **Touch All the Bases** introduces you to this time-honored sport which was first played in 1845. Baseball's heroes and legends have entertained and comforted Americans during good times and bad. The values prized in baseball, such as strategy, teamwork and sportsmanship, are also valued in business.

Whether you enjoy baseball, or know nothing about baseball, you will encounter baseball-related idioms and cultural references whenever you speak with Americans. So I invite you to read and listen to the story of Jey, a foreign-born American, as he learns about baseball and business.

Play Ball!
Jolinda Osborne

How to Get the Most from this Book

- Read the story at a leisurely pace. Take your time in order to understand all the expressions and cultural insights

- Refer to the Baseball Fundamentals on page 68 for an overview of the history and important of the game, for general rules, and for terminology that is used in the story.

- Listen to the audio. (See page 67 for download instructions.) You may want to listen while you read, or you may want to listen separately on your CD player while walking or traveling.

- Study the idioms **in bold** and the sample sentences at the bottom of each page to learn their meanings and business usage.

- Look up other words you don't understand. Useful dictionaries that allow you to listen to pronunciation are listed in the Resources section at the end of this book.

- Check out the Resources Section for more learning opportunities.

- Refer to the Index to see which idioms you remember, and which ones you'll want to review.

In the following fictional story, Jey, his wife, Shoba, and his son, Sammy, are a family from Asia who now live in Kansas City, Missouri. They face some of the same communication challenges that many non-native speakers face when encountering American idioms and cultural references at work, and at play.

Abbreviations used with the definitions:

    n. = noun   **v.** = verb   **adj.** = adjective   **adv.** = adverb

Touch All the Bases

See page 67 to download the free audio.

First Inning

Jey glanced at the **scoreboard** as he steered his car into the Harry S. Truman elementary school parking lot. Only one inning remained to be played in Sammy's baseball game, a game Jey had promised his son he would attend. Jey was running late because he had been detained at his office, located in a local high-tech industrial park. His impatient engineering team had initiated a lengthy discussion, during which they asked him to **step up to the plate** and make key design changes in the project that he was leading.

Inning – n. in baseball, a division in the game, wherein teams alternate who has an opportunity to score runs before making three "outs;" in business, a window of opportunity to act or speak out; a time-limited chance for accomplishment
- *"We're almost out of **innings**. It's 4 p.m., and we promised to deliver the project specs to the customer by the end of the day."*

Scoreboard – n. a large board, often near the outfield fence, that shows the hits, runs, and errors for both teams; in business, a means of tracking progress
- *"Our region by region **scoreboard** shows increasing sales in Asia."*

Step up to the plate – v. to stand at home plate and prepare to hit the pitched ball; in life or in business, to face a challenging situation
- *"He **stepped up to the plate** and volunteered for the dangerous, overseas assignment."*

Jey climbed the wooden **bleachers,** where his wife, Shoba, and a dozen other parents were cheering for Sammy's *Bears* and the opposing *Gophers* team.

Jey sat down, hoping Sammy wouldn't notice his late arrival, but his son, standing in centerfield, waved his oversized **glove** at his father. "**Better late than never**," Jey whispered to his wife. She pulled up her sleeve, looked at her wristwatch and silently scowled.

Baseball was a foreign and perplexing sport to Jey, and he didn't understand why Sammy wanted so badly to play baseball on the community **Little League** team. Why hadn't his son chosen to play soccer, an increasingly popular sport in America? Or tennis?

Bleachers – **n.** a tiered stand of wooden or metal seats and steps where spectators sit while watching a game

Glove – **n.** baseball equipment specially designed for fielding and catching a baseball

Better late than never – a phrase said in exasperation at a delay
- *"The bus arrived an hour late, but **better late than never**."*

Little League – **n.** Little League is a non-profit US-based organization which organizes youth baseball and softball leagues throughout the US and other parts of the world, particularly Asia and Latin America. In 2010 over two million boys and girls participated in Little League games.

Or **cricket**? Cricket was a sport Jey could get excited about. Plus, he would be able to give Sammy some tips — that is, if he ever found spare time from his grueling work schedule.

Sammy stood in the large, grassy outfield. He looked very small in his baggy blue and white *Bears* baseball uniform and **cap**. *B&D Exterminators* was written across the back of his uniform above the number **5**. Jey and Shoba had thought it strange than a local pest exterminator company would be the team's **sponsor**. However, Sammy and his teammates joked about how they would squash opponents like bugs and catch balls **on the fly**.

Suddenly Jey's cell phone rang loudly, audible even to Sammy in centerfield. Sammy knew the distinctive ring meant that his father would likely have to return to work. Sammy looked over at the bleachers where his father sat, and took his eyes off the game.

Crack! The **batter** for the opposing *Tasty Burger Gophers* hit a baseball that flew out into centerfield, bounced in front of Sammy, and then rolled through his legs.

Cricket – n. a sport played with balls and bats by teams of 11 players, popular in British Commonwealth countries. Good sportsmanship and adherence to proper etiquette are stressed. Thus if a behavior is not cricket, it is unfair.
- *"It's **not cricket** to take a second slice of cake at the birthday party until everyone has had a piece."*

Cap – n. a brimmed hat worn by baseball players, usually with a team logo
- *"At the awards banquet, our CEO gave out **caps** with our company logo."*

Sponsor – n. a person or organization that provides financial support
- *"We need to find a corporate **sponsor** to help with maintenance of our community park, or else it we'll have to close the park."*

On the fly – adv. catching the ball in flight; in a hurry, or doing something on the run
- *"I've got so much work to do that I'll have to eat lunch **on the fly**."*

Batter – n. a player whose turn it is to try to hit the ball

"Hey, don't be **caught napping**!" someone in the bleachers called out.

Sammy knew he should have caught the ball, or at least stopped it from rolling to the far fence, and he would have caught it if he had been paying more attention. Sammy raced after the ball and threw it back into the infield, but the *Gophers* scored because of his **error,** and **took the lead**. Once again, the *Bears* were about to lose the ball game.

Disgustedly, Sammy kicked the grass in front of him. "It could have happened to anyone!" Shoba called out loudly. She had learned a lot about baseball since attending all of Sammy's practice sessions and games. More importantly, she wasn't about to let anyone, even a well-meaning *Bears* parent, **razz** her son.

Shoba's spirited words of encouragement surprised Jey. His wife, a quiet, thoughtful person, usually said little in public, but there she sat in her colorful long skirt, cheering **with the best of them**. In fact, Jey was the only onlooker who *wasn't* focused on the game. He had scrambled down the risers to find a quiet spot where, on his cell phone, he talked with his research team

---

Caught napping – v. [passive] to have failed to respond because of inattention
- *"Our competitor took our best customer while we were **caught napping**."*

Error – n. a mistake made by a fielder

Take the lead – v. to be ahead in a game; to take leadership of something; also to overcome someone else
- *"At first we lagged behind other departments, but now our team has **taken the lead** in reducing manufacturing defects."*

Razz – v. to deride, heckle, tease, make fun of
- *"We won't tolerate any **razzing** of employees at our company."*

With the best of them – adv. as well as anyone else
- *"Jeff can photograph African wildlife **with the best of them**."*

as they **tossed around** an idea to modify the experiments that had failed in the test lab.

By the time Jey returned to his seat, the *Bears* were **at bat**. They had scored a run, two players were **on base** with hits, and Sammy was **on deck**. He had a chance to win the game for his team, if only he could get a base hit and drive home two of his teammates who stood on second and third base.

When the batter **struck out**, Sammy stepped up to the plate. He fixed his eyes on the ball as it left the **pitcher's** hand and spun toward him.

Toss around – v. to throw a ball around from one player to another; to discuss or debate an issue.
- *"The managers **tossed around** ideas for how to cut operating costs."*

At bat – adv. where a player has a chance to get a hit; thus, in a position to make something happen
- *"I see by the agenda that we're **at bat**; we have ten minutes to convince the room of investors that our start up company is worthy of financing."*

On base – adv. in baseball, to be in a safe position

On deck – adv. scheduled to bat next; available, ready to take action
- *"We've got a crew **on deck** to clean up after the trade show."*

Strike out – v. to fail to hit the ball when standing at the plate; thus, to fail in an endeavor or in an effort
- *"We **struck out** in our effort to produce a cheaper fuel source."*

Pitcher – n. the **pitcher** throws to the batter to start play in baseball; to **pitch** is to toss something; in business, to pitch is to attempt to promote or sell
- *"We **pitched** our new social networking idea to the Vice President."*

He wanted to smash the ball so that it would sail out beyond where the opposing *Gophers* players could catch it, over the distant white fence for a **home run**. He wanted to win the game for his fellow *Bears* teammates.

"Strike one!" the umpire shouted when Sammy swung his bat and missed the ball. Sammy missed the second pitch as well. "Strike two!" The parents of kids from both teams leaned forward in their seats. No one said a word. Sammy had **two strikes against him**.

Jey sucked in his breath. "You can do it, Sammy," he whispered. "You can get a hit."

On the third pitch, Sammy swung the bat so hard that the bat flew out of his hands and landed halfway down the first base line. But he missed the ball. "**Strike three**!" the umpire called. "You're out!" The game was over.

Sammy threw down his **batting helmet** and walked off to retrieve his bat. To **add insult to injury,** the other team's best player picked up Sammy's bat, dusted it off, and smiled smugly as he handed it back to Sammy.

Home Run – n. in baseball, a ball hit over the fence that allows the batter and any base runners to score; in business, a big success
- *"Kim scored a home run; he sold an acre of real estate for a 100% profit."*

Two strikes against [someone] – in a precarious or unenviable situation; in danger; about to lose
- *"The new book had **two strikes against it**: the book cover was ugly and the print was hard to read. No wonder it didn't sell well."*

Strike Three! – Sometimes used as in: "You've had your **three strikes**." A person has had three chances, and failed.
- *"The vendor got his **three strikes**; he failed to deliver the high-quality bolts and rivets to us that he promised. We won't use that vendor again."*

Batting helmet – n. protection for the batter against a pitched ball

Add insult to injury – v. to hurt a person's feelings after doing him harm; to make a bad situation worse
- *"**To add insult to injury**, after the newly-hired employee took over my office, he also got the promotion that I had been promised."*

"You'll do better next game," Shoba said as she climbed down the bleachers and approached Sammy.

Sammy shrugged off his mother's attempt to hug him. He and his fellow twelve-year-old teammates were embarrassed by public hugs and **pep talks** from their mothers. He pulled the brim of his cap down low over his brow and squeezed his eyes to prevent tears of frustration from trickling down his cheeks.

As he walked back to his mother's car, Sammy doubted he'd ever be a **clutch-hitter** and help his *Bears* win a baseball game. Although he usually contributed to his team with some good defensive fielding, his record for base hits was a **goose egg**. He had **gotten to first base** only because opponents bobbled the baseballs he hit to them, or else the opposing pitchers had **walked** him. Once on base, Sammy was a fast runner, but he wanted to earn his place as a base runner by getting a solid base hit.

On the drive home, Sammy stared out the car window and wondered if he should have listened to his father, who urged him to play a different sport. Several times, Sammy had tried to explain that his best friends at school played baseball, that baseball was called

---

Pep talk – n. a short speech to boost enthusiasm or improve morale
- *"The manager's **pep talk** inspired her salespeople to make an extra effort to get new orders despite the slow season."*

Clutch hitter – n. a player who gets a hit when runners are in scoring position; a person to be relied on to make an enterprise successful
- *Our project leader is a **clutch-hitter**; when we get stuck, he always comes up with a way to solve big problems and move the project forward."*

Goose egg – n. zero, especially when written numerically
- *"Income today from our open-air market stall was a **goose egg**."*

Get to first base – v. to achieve the first step; to succeed in the initial phase
- *"We **got to first base** in the tariff negotiations by agreeing on protocols."*

Walk – n. If a pitcher throws four balls outside the strike zone, a batter is allowed to go to first base without having to get a hit.

the **American pastime**, and that his friends traded **baseball cards** and talked at school lunch break about the best Major League professional players. However, his father always nodded without really understanding, and then returned to the mathematical formulas on his laptop.

American pastime – n. a term used to describe baseball. Baseball is one of the oldest organized sports. Baseball games are played in nearly all American cities (and in many countries around the world) at the professional, semi-professional, amateur and Little League levels. A pastime is a way of spending recreational or spare time in a pleasant manner.

Baseball card – n. cards, usually 2 ½ x 3 ½ inches with color photo or painting of a baseball player on one side, and statistics about that player on the other side. For decades these cards were sold with chewing gum products, and more recently with other candy or items. Today they are often traded online and saved by collectors. Many internet sites display collections of baseball cards, some going back a 100 years.

Second Inning

The next day in his cubicle at MedicMon, Jey pictured Sammy's strikeout over and over in his head, like an **instant replay**. After he witnessed his son's failure to hit the ball, and heard the crowd's groaning disappointment, Jey fled the ballpark and returned to work and his computer screen; he just couldn't bear to see his son so miserable. Jey realized that he was hopelessly **out of his league** in being able to console his son or help him achieve what would make him happy – success as a baseball player.

Jey found it hard to concentrate during the four meetings he attended before noon that day. He feared his project was **heading south**. His complex algorithm, to be included in a medical monitoring device code-named "Joltin' Joe," required re-testing and complex validation.

Instant replay – n. video of a sports play that is eplayed so viewers at home in front of their TVs or in the bleachers can see the play again and analyze the play
- *"Presentation training classes often use **instant replay** to show students how to improve the delivery of their presentations."*

Out of one's league – adv. beyond one's area of expertise or ability
- *"The office assistant was **out of his league** when he tried to do complex accounting."*

Head south – v. to go in the wrong direction; to go off course; to go bad
- *"Our cash flow situation is **heading south**. We'd better contact the bank to see if we can extend our line of credit."*

His internal customer, a demanding design team, was **playing hardball** by asking for more data for various usage models. Jey's research team had a lot of **moxie**, but they were simply short-staffed. In order to meet the team's commitments, some of the research work would need to be **farmed out**. Jey had to decide who he could call on for help; he needed someone who would be **fast out of the box**.

Adding to Jey's stress was a phone call early that morning from his teammate, Dave, co-author of Jey's latest patent application and co-developer of the algorithm feature they planned to present the following month to their Japanese partner. Dave had been **benched** by his doctor, who insisted Dave take an emergency medical leave due to a disturbing heart condition.

Play hardball – v. to act aggressively, sometimes ruthlessly or unethically
- *"Politicians often **play hardball** in their political ads just before an election."*

Moxie – n. courage, pluck, perseverance, showing confidence
- *"He showed a lot of **moxie** when deciding to open his own restaurant at a site where other restaurants had failed."*

Farm out – v. to assign something to an outsider or contractor. Baseball teams often have farm teams where they send potentially excellent young players to gain experience and confidence.
- *"I'm so busy that I need to **farm out** several clients to an associate."*

Fast out of the box – adj. describes a good start, [as a hitter running to first base]; thus, a quick learner
- *"The cashier I hired is **fast out of the box**; she learned in a day the prices of all our products."*

Bench – v. to take someone out of the game or out of the action; also, the reserve players on a team [who sit on a bench and wait]
- *"The hospital will have to **bench** the surgeon until his injured hand heals."*

Jey listened to Dave's story, wished him well, and then set down the phone. He realized he **had no one in the bull pen** to step in and relieve him of the extra work that loomed over him like a Midwestern thundercloud.

Jey reached into his desk drawer and felt around among the pens and paperclips for a pain pill to ease his worsening headache. Jey would have to **pinch hit** for Dave at the upcoming Senior Manager's meeting and present their status report, a report revealing that the project was behind schedule.

At noon, Jey cleared a spot on his cluttered desk and opened his backpack to find the lunch that Shoba packed for him that morning. The smell of her delicious spicy meals comforted him. He ate slowly, calm at last in the midst of another stressful day. He turned away from his computer screen, closed his eyes, and let his mind return to Sammy, his only child whom he loved so much that his heart ached when he thought of Sammy not being happy. In the quiet of his cubicle, an idea began to form, an idea as simple and complex as an elegant mathematical equation.

Jey pressed his fingers to his furrowed brow in order to think harder. Did his idea **have legs**? How could he possibly make it work? He knew rigor and organization would be called for, and he'd need to rely on his teammates **like never before**.

Have no one in the bullpen – **v.** to be without help; in baseball, relief pitchers come in from the bullpen (an area where a pitcher warms up his arm by pitching to teammates) when the starting pitcher is in trouble
- *"We **have no one in the bullpen** to handle new clients; all of our attorneys all busy on other major cases."*

Pinch hit – **v.** to step in to bat for another player; to substitute for
- *"The regular pizza delivery guy is sick; I had to **pinch hit** and drive the van."*

Have legs – **adj.** able to survive or thrive; good enough to succeed
- *"Our city park redesign plan **has legs**; the mayor and city council like it."*

Like never before – **adv.** more or better than what has previously existed
- *"At medical school I'm going to study **like never before** in order to become a doctor."*

He breathed deeply, as he'd been taught to breathe for yoga, and weighed his chances of success, as well as the consequences of failure. In his mind Jey outlined a way to re-align resources in order to complete the validation testing and free up more of his own time. To deliver the product feature on schedule, he'd have to use his influence to pull in every extra resource he could find.

Jey had a lot of **clout** with upper management because of his past performance successes, but in order to convince his boss, he would need a winning strategic **game plan**. Suddenly, he bolted upright in his chair, eyes now wide open; he stowed the remainder of his lunch in his pack and set to work. He gave himself a deadline: by the end of the day, he needed to create a convincing presentation to his manager, a MedicMon veteran, who would closely question any change in direction that seemed to **come out of left field**.

Jey's heart raced. It crossed his mind that he, like his colleague Dave, also had an aching heart; Jey's heart seemed to skip a beat whenever he pictured his son's disappointment. Jey resolved to **go to bat for** his son, no matter what effort and sacrifice it would require. His challenge was to do so and still keep his job.

Clout – n. power, strength or influence; in baseball, a hard hit
- *"The local business contractor has **clout** with the municipal government; he gets construction permits approved faster than anyone else in town."*

Game plan – n. a strategy, method of execution
- *"Our **game plan** is to distribute our fragrant beauty products through franchises."*

Come out of left field – v. to appear unexpectedly and without warning
- *"His resignation **came out of left field**; no one thought he would leave the company after being there for 25 years."*

Go to bat for – v. to actively support or help
- *"My supervisor **went to bat for** me when I was accused of causing the failure on the assembly line."*

Third Inning

"Oh, no," Jey moaned as another of his thrown baseballs landed in the dirt in front of home plate. Jey hadn't realized how difficult it was to pitch a small hard baseball over a white rubber "plate" 66 feet away, and keep it in the **strike zone**.

Sammy didn't swing at Jey's poor pitches, so at least his son was learning patience and discernment. Jey's next pitch sailed high and nearly **beaned** Sammy, who spun out of the way.

"Hey, Dad, don't kill your only son!" Sammy grinned, for although the batting practice hadn't resulted in any hits, he and his father were sharing a fun Saturday afternoon, a time his father usually spent at the office.

The Saturday practice session hadn't occurred by chance. Before sunrise that morning, Jey spent two hours on his laptop in the den. He **fielded** a dozen troubling emails in response to his Friday afternoon proposal to re-align the project. His manager had

---

Strike zone – n. the area over home plate where a pitch must be thrown to be called a strike; in business, a targeted area to measure success
- *"We're in the **strike zone** if our newly-designed gas furnaces achieve 96% efficiency."*

Bean – v. to hit the batter on the head with a pitched baseball

Field – v. in baseball, to retrieve the baseball after it has been hit by the batter; in business, to respond to questions from an audience or from customers
- *"Our customer service department is trained to **field** complaints, and to provide immediate help and satisfaction."*

expressed skepticism; he didn't like being **thrown a curve**. Jey's three teammates, Bob, Karl, and Yoko, had dashed off emails of concern about Jey's proposal. Specifically they wanted to know who would be **in the lineup** for the re-alignment. Jey knew that if he didn't handle his team properly he'd lose their loyalty. Most importantly, he would jeopardize the entire project if his proposal was **off-base**. Such a failure would squash his chances for a promotion at the end of the year.

Jey tried to wash away his own doubts while showering and shaving. When he greeted his family in the kitchen for breakfast, he had regained confidence in his plan. Jey ate some spicy rice and vegetables, and then poured Sammy a bowl of **Wheaties®,** a cereal with **"Breakfast of Champions"** written on the orange box. Lately, Sammy wanted to eat only American food: cereal, sandwiches, pizza, and a fair amount of snack food. A **tug of war** often ensued between Sammy and Shoba, who insisted that he at least eat her traditional Asian meals at dinner.

Throw a curve – **v.** to surprise, fool, or outmaneuver someone
- *"My son **threw me a curve** when he announced he had found a job outside of our family business."*

Lineup – **n.** players in the game; people on a team; a selection of products
- *"Our clothing company has a new hire; she will add graphic arts expertise to our **lineup** of fabric designers."*

Off-base – **adj.** in baseball, not on the base, so liable to be called out; not correct, not legal, not workable
- *"The scientist's theory is **off-base**; it is based on incorrect laboratory data."*

Wheaties, Breakfast of Champions™ – **n.** a popular American breakfast cereal of flaked wheat that is eaten with milk. The front of the box has a picture a sports star, while the back of the box gives information about that player.

Tug of war – **n.** a contest of strength in which two teams tug on ends of a rope and try to pull the other team across a dividing line; a struggle for supremacy
- *"We're in a **tug of war** with our competitor to determine who will dominate the racing bicycle market segment."*

Jey sipped his breakfast tea as he announced the two errands he had planned for the morning. He enjoyed the surprised look on Sammy's face, and the energy with which Sammy finished his breakfast and washed up.

First they drove to the neighborhood public library where Jey nearly **cleaned out** the shelf of books on baseball. He was amazed by the number of books on hitting, pitching, catching, strategy, and scorekeeping. Baseball was one of America's oldest sports, and books chronicled every aspect of the game's history, strategy, and players.

Then they visited a sports store where Jey bought two bats, another glove, and a box of baseballs. At Sammy's urging, Jey also purchased a **New York Yankees** cap. The Yankees were Sammy's favorite **Major League** team.

By the time they reached the school baseball **diamond**, Jey and Sammy looked like any other father and son out for some weekend batting practice. Only an observer watching from the bleachers would have noticed that Jey knew practically nothing about baseball.

Clean out – v. to empty of contents; to leave bare
- *"In anticipation of the snowstorm, customers **cleaned out** our supply of water, snow shovels, and batteries."*

New York Yankees – Arguably, the Yankees are the most famous and successful Major League baseball team. As of 2011 the Yankees have won 27 World Series Championships. Famous Yankees include: Babe Ruth, Lou Gehrig, Joe DiMaggio, and Mickey Mantle, Yogi Berra, and Jessie Jackson.

Major League – major league teams field the best professional baseball players and are located in large American cities, as opposed to minor league teams located in smaller cities, where young and unproven players are seasoned; in business, major league defines something important or significant
- *"Our consulting firm gained a **major league** international banking client."*

Diamond – n. the field upon which baseball is played, so called because of the diamond shape of the infield

Baseball Diamond
Position of the Players and Umpire

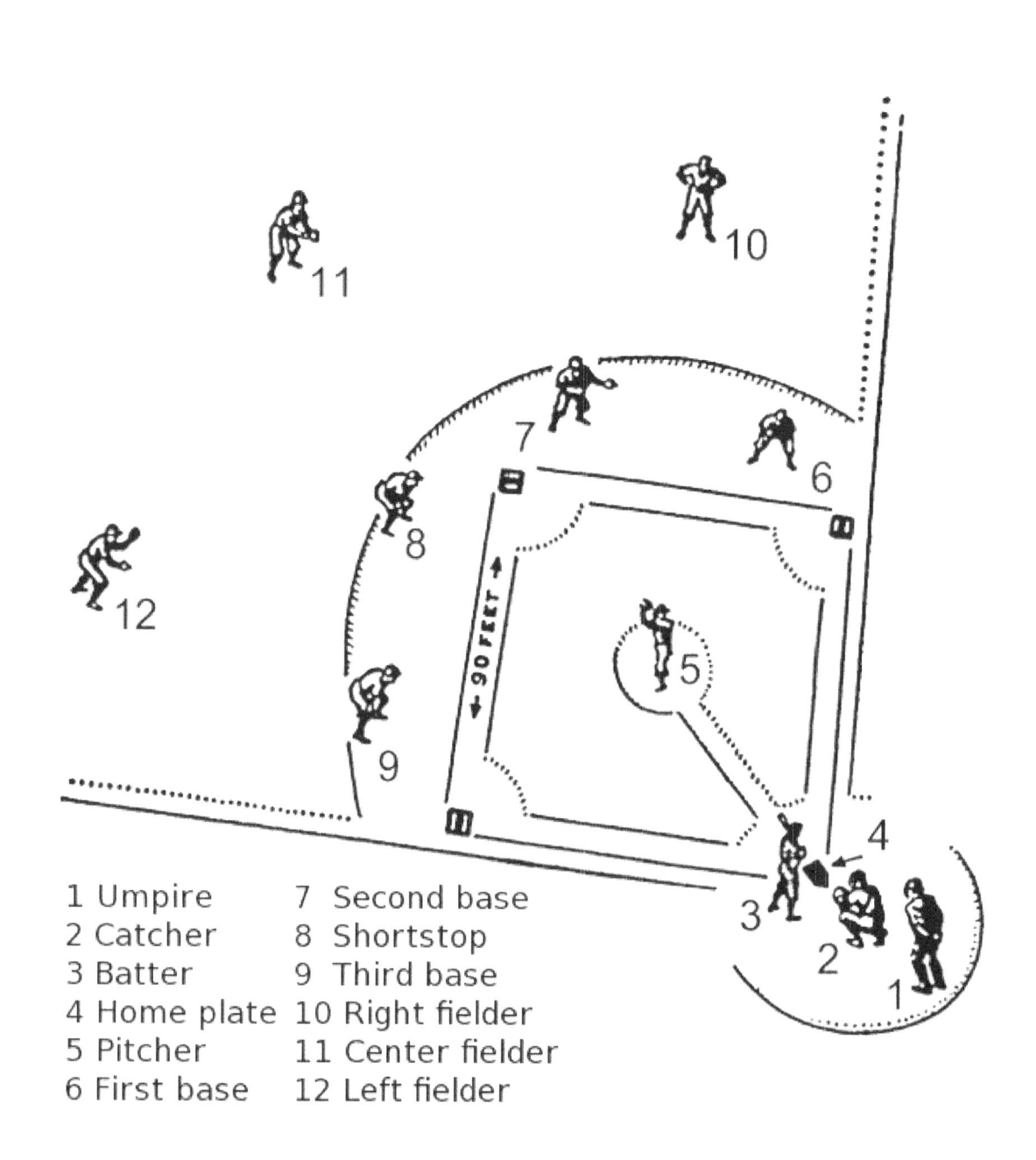

1 Umpire
2 Catcher
3 Batter
4 Home plate
5 Pitcher
6 First base
7 Second base
8 Shortstop
9 Third base
10 Right fielder
11 Center fielder
12 Left fielder

As the sun climbed high into the sky and the humidity of a Missouri afternoon made his shirt cling to his back, Jey took off his cap to wipe his sweaty brow. He began to think that he'd **come up with** the dumbest idea of his life. How, in order to help his son, could he learn enough skills about a sport he previously dismissed as being boring? How, at the same time, could he carve out enough time to successfully complete the critical project at work, a project that could **make or break** his career and the fortunes of his company? Both goals seemed hopelessly out of reach.

Then, *Crack!*

Sammy hit the ball! The ball soared high and long out into centerfield. Sammy hit the ball! Jey beamed as Sammy jumped for joy and ran to retrieve the ball and toss it back. Jey caught the ball and felt the solid weight of it in his glove; he **had to admit** that it felt good.

Jey pitched another baseball. *Crack!*

They practiced another hour. Sammy continued to hit the ball, often on the **sweet spot** of the bat, while Jey became more skilled at fielding the ball as it was hit back to him. The key to fielding, Jey realized, was getting the glove down low so that the ball didn't roll beneath the glove and through his legs.

Come up with – *v.* to devise, create, or think up
- "We need to **come up with** an attractive company logo that will work with both our online and print marketing strategies."

Make or break – *v.* to result in great success or complete failure
- "This holiday season will **make or break** us; we must sell all the inventory on our shelves or we're out of business."

Have to admit – *v.* to acknowledge something despite a reluctance to do so
- "I doubted the new receptionist would be a good employee, but I **have to admit** I was wrong. She's great at greeting customers and remembering names."

Sweet spot – *n.* a place on the bat where it's most effective to hit the ball; anything optimally designed for success
- "The **sweet spot** in our product line is our low-priced beer."

Jey learned to **keep his eye on the ball**. It was advice he'd heard Sammy's coach give every *Bears* player, and one of **the fundamentals** of baseball stressed by all the books he had skimmed while at the library.

Then without warning, dark clouds rolled in, a sign that foretold a coming thunderstorm. Jey hadn't yet adapted to the extremes of Missouri weather: the snow and wind of winter, the steamy hot summers, and the sudden thunderstorms that could disrupt a June day.

Jey and Sammy raced for the car as large-sized hail suddenly fell from the sky. They sat a moment in the closed car, their breath steaming the windows, and listened to the hail beat against the car roof. Then Jey carefully steered the car homeward, his windshield wipers going at full speed. He felt grateful for his substantial car, for his comfortable home, and for the opportunities his adopted country had given him to provide for his family and expand his career. He found himself humming a childhood song as he contemplated the hot, delicious meal Shoba would have waiting for them.

Keep one's eye on the ball – **v.** to remain alert, attentive and focused; good advice for a player of any sport that uses a ball
- "Each employee is instructed to **keep his eye on the ball** *in order to ensure that we don't have any injuries on the assembly line.*"

The fundamentals – **n.** whatever is essential or necessary
- "***The fundamentals*** *are in place for economic growth: low inflation and high consumer confidence.*"

That night, after an exhausted but joyful Sammy fell into bed, Jey applied a cold pack to his arm and collapsed in his **La-Z-Boy™** chair. His arm ached from all the pitches he had thrown. Shoba rubbed soothing ointment on the arm and across his lower back, but he knew he would be sore for days. He had never experienced such a physically challenging day; he realized that baseball required him to **be in** better **shape**.

Jey had never played sports in school. His youth was devoted to developing his mind. He worked diligently in high school to win a national mathematics competition and then a coveted university scholarship. When he became the youngest assistant professor at his city's university, he felt as if he were **in seventh heaven**.

However, the sudden death of both his parents meant he had to support his three younger brothers, and so, with great sadness and trepidation, he left the **friendly confines** of the university for a larger salary, and for more pressure with an American high-technology company situated in his hometown.

La-Z-Boy ™ – n. popular brand of padded, recliner chairs often placed in front of the TV. Many different companies make similarly-styled chairs, but the name La-Z-Boy has become synonymous with a comfortable spot to view a baseball or other sports game.

In shape – adj. physically fit; in a state of readiness or good condition
- *"Finally our patent application **is in shape** for the company lawyers to review."*

In seventh heaven – adv. in a state of great joy and satisfaction
- *"My friends are **in seventh heaven**; they just bought their dream home and had their first baby."*

Friendly confines – n. a term for the home team's baseball stadium; a comfortable place in which to work
- *"I think most clearly in the **friendly confines** of my upstairs office."*

Two years later, with a new wife and baby **in tow**, Jey found himself resettled in the heartland of the United States — Kansas City, Missouri — at the company's American headquarters.

"Jey. Jey." Shoba shook him awake. "You'll cramp your neck if you sleep all night in that chair."

Jey roused himself from a dream. In the dream he was running the wrong way around the bases in a uniform with his company's logo, waving a book of algorithms as the umpire **sent him to the showers**. He eased his sore body out of the chair; it was definitely time to go to bed.

In tow – **adv.** in one's charge
- *"The foreman took the new carpenter **in tow** and showed him all the project sites and tool sheds he'd need to know about."*

Send someone to the showers – **v.** to remove from the game or from the action. A baseball umpire has authority to remove a player from a game if the player breaks a rule or acts in an unprofessional manner.
- *"One member of our negotiation team showed his anger, so we **sent him to the showers**; his attitude jeopardized the negotiation."*

Fourth Inning

The following week, Jey **gave one hundred and ten percent** to managing his team, pushing forward his project, and writing his patent application. In two weeks he needed to present his completed methodology and algorithm, which he hoped would be embedded into a software feature co-designed by MedicMon's Japanese partner. He wanted to have the patent disclosure written before the important meeting in Japan in order to protect his company's intellectual property.

Jey wasn't really surprised when his manager **made the hard call** and told Jey that the project deadline couldn't be pushed back. Somehow, Jey and his team would have to complete the project on time and without help from Dave, who was at home recovering from heart surgery.

Give one hundred and ten percent – v. to exert more effort and energy than is expected, but which may be necessary for success
- *"Emily worked night and day to establish her online clothing design company. She knew she had to **give one hundred and ten percent** to her business if she expected to succeed."*

Make the hard call – v. to make a difficult, often emotional decision
- *"The VP **made the hard call** to lay off 20 employees because of the worsening recession."*

A successful project, his manager said, was the division's **meal ticket** to increased research funding. Jey sighed when he got the news; the additional demands at work would make it harder than ever to practice baseball with Sammy and attend his Little League games.

Wednesday afternoon arrived like a **fastball**. There was no way he could get away from work and arrive at the school for the start of Sammy's game. Jey had managed to finagle more resources for the project. Now a **rookie** from another department sat in Jey's cubicle, ready to validate some of the data for the experiment, but in need of supervision. Before he left the office, Jey also had to **touch base with** Yoko and Karl on another specification change from the design engineers.

Within minutes of driving out of the MedicMon parking lot, Jey was in rush hour traffic in the expanding high-technology area of Kansas City. In just two years Jey had noticed an influx of people and businesses all eager to take advantage of the city's entrepreneurial spirit, central location as a transportation hub of the country, and cultural amenities. With growth, however, came traffic.

Meal ticket – n. a source of financial support
- *"An insurance salesman's **meal ticket** consists of the commissions he receives for policy renewals."*

Fastball – n. a pitch thrown at up to 100 miles per hour in the hope that the batter will not be able to hit it

Rookie – n. an untrained or inexperienced person; a new hire; in baseball, a first year professional player
- *"The **rookie** accountant just out of college shows promise; soon we'll assign her an important client."*

Touch base with – v. to renew contact or communicate with; in baseball, a runner must touch the bases while advancing around the diamond
- *"Though I finished my Ph.D. program two years ago, I **touched base with** my former professor last month and got some good advice from him."*

When Jey finally arrived at the school parking lot, he understood the baseball idiom, **two down, one to go**. He had solved the problem of the technical experiment and the design requirements, and he had navigated the city traffic. Now he could focus on Sammy's game. He didn't want to admit to himself, however, that attending a baseball game was still a duty. He wished he felt more like his wife who genuinely had come to enjoy the American pastime.

The scoreboard behind centerfield showed that the opposing team, the *Handy Hardware Wolves,* had two runs, while Sammy's *Bears* had **no runs, no hits, no errors**. Although Sammy hadn't gotten a hit, Jey was relieved to see that at least he hadn't made any errors. Jey raced up the wooden bleachers and found a spot next to Shoba. With barely a glance his way, she poured him a cup of tea and pointed to the *Bears* players who were **in scoring position**, and to Sammy, who was on deck.

Nervous perspiration formed on Jey's brow. He could feel the excitement of the crowd. He now knew enough about baseball to realize that Sammy's *Bears* actually had a good chance to win the game. Sammy would soon **be up**, with the pressure on him to get a hit. Jey's stomach churned.

Two down one to go – two of three outs have been completed; in general, almost complete
- *"I worked all night on the financial reports; I've got **two down one to go**, and I hope to finish the last report by noon today."*

No runs, no hits, no errors – summary of a half inning of play when nothing of significance occurred in the baseball game; nothing to report

In scoring position – adv. within reach of success; close to achieving one's goal; in baseball, runners are positioned on 2nd or 3rd base, ready to come home
- *"The rock band's new CD has been a big success, and now they're **in scoring position** to sign a lucrative contract with a big record label."*

Be up – v. to be the next batter; to be next in line to take action
- *"Joan, the agenda shows that you **are up** next. Please give us your status report."*

Jason, the *Bears* best hitter and one of Sammy's friends, stood at the plate and faced the *Wolves* pitcher. Jason was **good in the clutch**, but this time at bat he struck out on three pitches from the opponent's lanky, strong pitcher.

The *Bears* fans, mainly parents, groaned in unison when Jason struck out. Jason's stern father hollered a swear word and slammed his coffee mug on the wooden seat. Shoba spun around to where he sat high in the bleachers, and she reminded him that the game was a family event, and that the children didn't appreciate such unsuitable language. Then she muttered loud enough for all to hear that such behavior gave all **Little League parents** a bad reputation. Jason's father simply crossed his arms and sulked.

"That *Wolves* pitcher **has got something on the ball**," Shoba remarked to Jey. After watching plenty of baseball, she had come to appreciate a talented baseball player, even if that talent was

---

Good in the clutch – adj. able to make the important play or take action under pressure or in a critical situation
- *"The attorney is **good in the clutch**; he always comes up with arguments that convince the jury to find his client innocent, even when the prosecutor's evidence seems overwhelming."*

Little League parents – Some Little League parents have a bad reputation because they show poor sportsmanship.
- *"The gymnast's mother reacted like a **Little League parent** to the poor score her daughter received from the judges."*

Have something on the ball – adj. especially capable, efficient or talented; the description of a pitcher who throws a pitched ball that hitters can't hit
- *"That medical intern **has something on the ball**; she diagnosed the patient's rare illness before the laboratory test results were completed."*

displayed by a boy of the opposing team. Jey was proud of the way his wife demonstrated good **sportsmanship**.

Then Sammy walked to the plate. Once again Jey noticed how small his son looked in his baseball uniform. Sammy put on an oversized, protective batting helmet and took a few practice swings to **loosen up**, just as Jey had taught him to do from reading one of the library books. Sammy appeared more relaxed than the parents, who fidgeted in their seats.

"You can do it, son," Jey whispered. "Just remember the fundamentals."

"Strike one!" the umpire yelled as Sammy swung wildly and **missed** the ball **by a country mile.** "Strike two!" Again Sammy swung at the pitch, and missed.

Jey gripped the thermos cup so hard that it flipped out of his hand, spilling the tea on his pants, before bouncing off the seat. Jey bent over to retrieve the cup.

Crack.

Jey jerked his head up and looked toward where Sammy stood at the plate, just as the foul ball that Sammy had hit sailed into the bleachers – and landed on Jey's nose.

Dazed, Jey blinked at the pain as blood spurted out and dripped onto his khaki pants. Everyone in the bleachers looked stunned. Shoba quickly held a handkerchief to his nose to stem the

---

Sportsmanship – n. conduct and attitude when playing sports; good sportsmanship involves fair play, courtesy, and grace when losing
- *"We showed good **sportsmanship** and congratulated our competitor who won the airplane engine contract with the lowest bid.*

Loosen up – v. to reduce tension in the muscles; slang for "take it easy"
- *""Don't worry about the presentation; just **loosen up** and relax, and speak from your heart."*

Miss by a country mile – v. to miss by a very large margin; to make an obvious mistake or misjudgment
- *"We forecasted quarterly profits of $1.5 million, but we **missed by a country mile**. We actually lost money this past quarter."*

blood, while several parents pulled cold packs from their **coolers** so that Jey could **ice down** his swelling nose.

"What happened?" Jey muttered. He didn't quite comprehend the reason his nose hurt so badly.

"Be still," Shoba said as she applied more ice.

On the field, Sammy was momentarily delighted that he hit the ball. His grin disappeared, however, when he turned to look at the commotion in the **stands** and saw his Dad's face. He started to run toward Jey, but the umpire caught Sammy's sleeve.

"Play ball," the umpire reminded both Sammy and the pitcher. When the next pitch came, Sammy swung the bat and **knocked one out of the box** past the first baseman for his first base hit as a Little League player.

"That's my Sammy!" Shoba shouted gleefully, and then affectionately nudged Jey with her elbow. "Sammy got a *hit* and you *got* hit."

Jey didn't know whether the tears that welled in his eyes came from his painful nose or from the pride he was feeling as he watched his son standing on first base. He continued to hold ice to his nose while watching the remainder of the game.

Coolers – n. insulated containers, often taken to ball games or picnics, for keeping food and drinks cold

Ice down – v. to put ice on an injury in order to reduce swelling

Stands – n. bleachers at a playing field or stadium

Knock one out of the box – v. to hit the ball hard; to be successful
- *"I'm sure our division will **knock one out of the box** with the newly-designed infant car seat we're introducing to the market next month."*

Unfortunately, Sammy was **stranded** on first when the following batters grounded out, so the *Bears* lost the game.

As Jey made his way gingerly down the bleacher steps for a trip to the hospital emergency room, he overheard the *Bears* coach tell the team, "You boys did fine today. Remember **it's not whether you win or lose, but how you play the game**."

Good advice for youngsters playing Little League, Jey thought. He wished the advice was accepted in the business world. At his company, winning was imperative and losing could be fatal. In business, Jey knew he could **be at the top of his game** one week, but if he couldn't successfully deliver his project on time, he would likely **be sent down to the minors**.

Jey's head ached, and he worried that his nose was broken because he couldn't breathe through it. His immediate concern, however, was whether his injury would prevent him from returning to work later that night.

Stranded – v. [passive] to be left on base and unable to score a run; to be left without help or rescue
- *"Because of bad weather, I was **stranded** at the airport and couldn't make the important meeting."*

It's not whether you win or lose but how you play the game – often-cited advice that emphasizes effort and sportsmanship over winning

At the top of one's game – adv. at the height of one's ability, achievement, or success
- *"The physician is **at the top of her game**; she is one of the most respected brain surgeons in the country."*

Sent down to the minors – v. to be demoted, punished, have one's responsibilities reduced. The Minor League isn't as important as the Major League in baseball or other sports.
- *"If I don't complete the architectural design for the new library on time, I'll **be sent down to the minors** and will only get to design garages."*

In order to drive Jey to the hospital, Shoba allowed Sammy to go out with his teammates for **hot dogs** and soft drinks, even though she really did not like him to eat this kind of American fast food. Once she and Jey were assured that other parents would bring Sammy home after dinner, they drove off to the hospital, aware again of the complexities of earning a living in America and raising a son in two cultures.

Hot dog – n. a sausage made of pork, beef, chicken or, in certain modern ballparks, tofu, and served in a long, soft bun. Ballparks are noted for their hot dogs; used idiomatically, a person who shows off
- *"Ed is a **hot dog** when it comes to steering his motorboat along the river. He cuts in front of sailboats and comes too close to shore. One of these days he'll overturn his own motorboat and land in the water."*

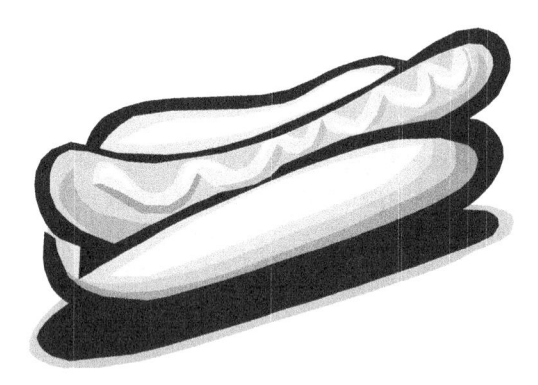

Fifth Inning

The following morning Jey appeared at the office **sporting** two black eyes and a white bandage covering his broken nose. He expected good-natured jokes accusing him of having run into a door, or being downright blind. He didn't anticipate, however, his colleagues' stories of their own baseball injuries: sprained fingers, strained backs, broken kneecaps, and bruises suffered to the most private of body parts. Everyone, it seemed, had a baseball **tale** to share.

As colleagues crowded around him in the café, Jey experienced a closeness to them that he had not felt since arriving in America. Sports were always the favorite subject of conversation at coffee

---

Sporting – v. [to sport] wearing or displaying something with the intention of being noticed
- *"One of our employees jokingly **sported** a T-shirt with our competitor's logo; we made him change shirts immediately."*

Tale – n. an entertaining story, often with a mix of truth and exaggeration
- *"When Joe returned a week late from his business trip, he told us a fabulous **tale** of why he was so late. He certainly had an amazing adventure, though we weren't sure if he was telling us the truth."*

breaks. **Right off the bat**, someone would bring up the previous day's news from the **sports page** – sparking a lively discussion of whatever sport was in season.

Jey inevitably felt left out because he didn't know anything about American sports. He usually nodded without comprehending, and then quietly walked away. That morning, however, he basked in the glow of his own story, which became exaggerated in the re-telling.

By the time the group finished their coffee and tea and scattered for a day of meetings, Jey knew more about his colleagues' families and personal lives than he'd learned in two years. Moreover, Steve, a medical engineer who usually talked with Jay only about technology, offered Jey two tickets to the Friday evening's **professional baseball game** between the Kansas City Royals and the famous New York Yankees.

Steve said a project deadline would keep him at work all weekend. Jey hesitated, for he also had work deadlines, but then he thought of how thrilled Sammy would be at the chance to watch the **pros** play. He reasoned that he would take along his laptop and get work done while Sammy watched the game.

Right off the bat – adv. immediately, instantly
- *"I can't answer your technical question **right off the bat**, but I'll get do some research and get back to you with an answer."*

Sports page – n. a section in the newspaper or online with the sports news

Professional baseball game – The **Kansas City Royals** and the **New York Yankees** are two of 15 teams in the American League. Other famous teams such as the Boston Red Sox are in the National League. Together the Leagues have 30 teams. Each team plays 162 games in a season. Then, depending upon who ranks highest in the number of winning games at the end of the season, teams play post-season games and, finally, the World Series, where the top two teams from each League compete to be World Champions.

Pro – n. short for professional; a person recognized as having expertise
- *"We've hired a **pro** to add more light and ambience to our restaurant."*

Sixth Inning

A blue, cloudless sky welcomed the fans who streamed into Kauffman Stadium that Friday after work. Sammy's eyes bulged at the sights and sounds of the boisterous crowd – **fans** of every age and background who converged to watch the hometown Royals take on the legendary Yankees.

Sammy wanted to **cheer on** his Yankees; however, the tickets they had received from Steve were for seats high up in the stadium amidst the Royals fans, so it seemed disloyal, even provocative, to wear his Yankee cap. Sammy stowed the cap in their backpack, and Jey purchased a Royals cap and an **Official Program** so they could read about the ball players. Sammy had insisted they take their gloves in case a foul ball flew their way and they could catch it for

---

Fan – n. an ardent devotee; an enthusiast
- *"I'm a **fan** of National Public Radio; I listen to it at home and in my car on the way to work."*

Cheer on – v. to encourage or actively support
- *"My communications coach **cheered me on** when I delivered a presentation at the city-wide conference."*

Official Program – n. A magazine-style program available at ball games that contains information about the teams, in particular the line-up and statistics on player performance

a souvenir. Jey, whose nose was still bandaged and sore, decided he would get out of the way of any balls that flew too close to him. He had no desire to **make a grandstand play**.

When Jey pulled his laptop from the pack, Sammy **rolled his eyes** in disbelief. Sammy pointed out that avoiding foul balls meant paying close attention, but Jey figured he could multi-task. "I'll **catch** the important plays," he confidently told his son.

As it turned out, Jey didn't get any work done that afternoon. A deafening roar from the crowd greeted the players who ran onto the field before the start of the game. The fans yelled and clapped and stomped their feet in support of their Royals, and then a few of them gave the visiting Yankees, who wore their traditional pinstripe uniforms, the **Bronx cheer**.

The crowd grew silent only when standing to hear the **National Anthem** sung by a local celebrity, but then the shouting resumed and rock music blared through the sound system.

Make a grandstand play – v. to show off or act ostentatiously; first used in baseball to describe a play made to look more difficult than it really is in order to win applause from the fans in the grandstand
- *"John **made a grandstand** play at the company picnic. He took charge of the fire extinguisher and rolled out the water hose, even though the small flame was merely from meat fat spattering on the BBQ grill."*

Roll one's eyes – v. to signal disbelief, astonishment, or mild disapproval
- *"The driver explained in great detail why he was speeding, but the policeman just **rolled his eyes** as he wrote out a ticket."*

Catch – v. to understand something, usually quickly or in small parts [catch has many other meanings]
- *"My cell phone reception is poor, but I **catch** the main points of your message."*

Bronx cheer – n. a loud sound made with the lips and tongue that expresses disapproval at players or umpires who disappoint or angers the fans. The Bronx is a section of New York where the Yankees have their stadium.

National Anthem – n. The Star-Spangled Banner is the name of the American National Anthem. Fans stand and sing it (sometimes with guest singers) before the start of baseball games, as well as at most other sporting events.

The **hawkers** yelled out *"Beer here, beer here, ice cold beer," "Peanuts, hot roasted peanuts"*, and *"Hot dogs, hot dogs,"* as they strolled up and down the cement grandstand steps carrying food heaped in giant baskets. The cacophony of sounds surged and ebbed like the roar of ocean waves breaking on the shore – ceaseless yet oddly exhilarating.

By Jey's **ballpark estimate**, 40,000 screaming fans in blue and white hats and Royals T-shirts filled the stadium. People swayed to the music and waved their hand-painted signs that supported the Royals, or occasionally the Yankees. Jey had never seen so many people gathered for one purpose – to enjoy themselves on a hot, humid, Missouri evening. Jey bought Sammy an ice cream bar before settling in for the start of the game.

Jey pulled his laptop from its case, but before he could open it, a kid in the row of seats behind him splashed his cup of soda on the laptop. People jostled Jey as they took their seats or passed money to the hawkers, who then passed back hot dogs that dripped ketchup and mustard. Horrified that he would damage his precious laptop, Jey wiped the lid off with his shirtsleeve and put the laptop safely back in the pack. He realized that bringing his laptop to a crowded ball game had been a mistake; he'd **chalk that up to experience**.

Hawker – n. a person who tries to sell something by shouting to get attention
- *"I was amused and frustrated when I tried to walk through a bazaar in Istanbul because **hawkers** kept calling out to me to buy their goods."*

Ballpark estimate/figure – n. a guess, an estimate
- *"In your project proposal, please provide exact costs; a **ballpark estimate** won't satisfy the finance department."*

Chalk something up to experience – v. to learn from one's mistake and move forward with better understanding
- *"As a new employee, I make lots of mistakes, but my manager tells me to **chalk them up to experience**."*

Sammy noticed his father fidgeting with his cell phone. "Hey, Dad, just **hang loose**. With all this noise you won't be able to hear the guys at the office anyway."

Sammy was right. Jey snapped shut his cell phone. He could bemoan the fact that he had so much work to do and was wasting time in a noisy stadium watching unknown teams play a sport he knew so little about. Or, he could listen to his son, and **take a breather** from the stress of work. The fans seemed to be able to unwind. Why couldn't he?

Jey became curious as to what millions of Americans, for over 150 years, had found so satisfying in the game being played on the bright green grass below. The scientist in him suddenly saw a question for investigation. Jey leaned forward. He was a life-long learner. Perhaps there was something to be learned by observing the game of baseball.

As players came to the plate in the first inning, Sammy studied the Program for **stats** on the players. Jey was pleased by Sammy's sudden interest in players' **batting averages**, number of runs scored, percentage of hits with men in scoring position, and a dozen others

---

Hang loose – v. slang for "take it easy," relax
- *"The lab experiment failed, but I suggest we **hang loose** and try to think of what went wrong."*

Take a breather – v. take a break, relax
- *"We've been working for ten hours straight. Let's **take a breather** and listen to some music."*

Stats – n. short for statistics; in baseball, various measurements of hitting and fielding performance by ball players
- *"We need the **stats** on assembly line defects so that we can address the root cause of the problem and fix it."*

Batting average – n. performance of hitters obtained by dividing the number of hits by the total number of times at bat; performance
- *"Our company's **batting average** is slipping; we haven't released our usual five new products this year."*

statistics. Jey hoped his son was finally **showing a talent for** mathematics. In school, Sammy excelled in geography and English, but his math grade, to Jey's shock and disappointment, was just above average.

Jey **looked over Sammy's shoulder** at the printed program. Mentally he calculated who on the opposing team was likely to get a hit. Baseball, he realized, could be seen as **a numbers game**. Jey considered the number 3, a prime number: three strikes before a batter was called out; three outs before teams changed sides; 3 x 3 = nine innings of play.

But there were also plenty of "fours": four balls thrown by the pitcher allowed the hitter to get on base; four bases set out in geometric harmony of 90 degree angles [a diamond] to form a 360 degree whole, a challenge to a player who had to round those bases and get "home" in order to score. The dynamism of 3, and the completeness of 4. How elegant and balanced the game of baseball was, Jey thought.

The dual of opposites was also evident in every play: pitcher against batter. One man's job was to pitch the ball with sizzling precision and keep it away from the batter; the other man's task was to make contact with that small, speeding ball and hit it where no one would catch it.

Show a talent for – v. to exhibit innate ability, talent or potential
- *"Sergei **shows a talent for writing**; his short story was printed in a major, prestigious literary magazine."*

Look over someone's shoulders – v. to scrutinize or pay close attention; to micro-manage someone
- *"I always make mistakes when the boss **looks over my shoulder**."*

A numbers game – n. slang for a way of looking at betting, games, or life by figuring out the odds
- *"The life insurance industry is really **a numbers game**; premiums are figured on the average of how many people will die in a given time span."*

Often the outcome of this **game of inches** was determined when a ball **took a bad bounce,** or a sudden breeze blew a **fair ball** inches foul, or a pitch crossed the plate just outside the strike zone, or a well-hit baseball soared inches above a fielder's outstretched glove.

When players made a daring or difficult play, as Jey and Sammy witnessed from their seats each inning, the crowd roared its approval. But when a fielder was **off his game** and bobbled the ball or **choked** at the plate, that failure was public and his

Game of inches – n. a game or situation in which the slightest variation is important; an arena or field of work where accuracy is critical
- *"Making medical instruments is **a game of inches**. It requires precise measurements."*

Take a bad bounce – v. when a baseball bounces in a way that is unexpected, it might lead to an error; thus, to lead to a miscalculation or unwelcome outcome
- *"Relations with our union employees **took a bad bounce** when we brought up new health insurance issues in our negotiations."*

Fair ball – n. a ball that is in play, meaning that the runners may advance and the fielders can try to make an out

Off one's game – adj. not working or functioning at one's best; not in top form
- *"Sherry is a great chef, but she was **off her game** last night. She overcooked the fish and undercooked the cakes."*

Choke – v. to fail to perform effectively because of nervousness or tension
- *"The technician **choked** when he was asked to demonstrate the new technology to the CEO. He couldn't get the hardware or the software to work."*

alone to bear. The crowd would then shout "**bush-league**!" Or worse.

Jey took in the whole of the playing field, and he saw the game as a reflection of the American business culture he'd been living and working in for two years. Heightened expectancy was followed by a spurt of action, either successful or not, either brilliant or routine, and then the game returned to a state of tense waiting until the next play unfolded.

Another similarity was that although both baseball and business recognized the importance of teamwork, responsibility for precise execution rested with the individual. At work, as at the ballpark, the individual won or lost the game. The individual was accountable—the day's hero or **bum**. That realization made Jey check his cell phone. Two messages from Yoko blinked on the screen.

Bush-league – adj. not of a professional standard; inadequate or unsophisticated, as if coming from the countryside (the bushes)
- *"Our mayor failed to persuade the company to relocate to our city because her inadequate economic incentives were criticized as being **bush-league**."*

Bum – n. an incompetent, lazy, useless person. Sometimes baseball fans call their team members **"bums"** when they don't perform as expected.

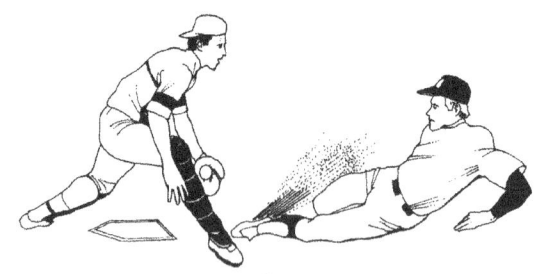

Seventh Inning

Before Jey could plug in his headset to retrieve his messages, however, the stadium announcer called on everyone in the crowd to join in the **Seventh Inning Stretch**. Fans stood and sang baseball's signature song, *Take Me Out to the Ball Game*, as it blared over the loudspeaker.

> *Take me out to the ball game*
> *Take me out with the crowd.*
> *Buy me some peanuts and* **Cracker Jack**,
> *I don't care if I never get back.*
> *Let me root, root, root for the home team,*
> *If they don't win it's a shame!*
> *For it's one, two, three strikes you're out!*
> *At the Old Ball Game.*

"Can we have a hot dog, Dad?" Sammy asked as they stood to stretch their legs. "I won't tell Mom."

Jey signaled to the hot dog concessionaire who walked by. Jey handed him a $10 bill and bought two hot dogs. He had to admit he was hungry, and the plump hot dogs dripping with condiments smelled so good. Jey decided he wouldn't think about what went into

---

Seventh Inning Stretch - n. a pause midway through the seventh inning of play when fans stand to stretch their legs, get snacks, and sing baseball's famous 1927 song; any break in the action
- *"Negotiations aren't going well, so I suggest we take a **seventh inning stretch**."*

Cracker Jack™ – n. a trademarked brand of caramel-coated popcorn with peanuts, sold in small boxes with a prize inside; used idiomatically, the term means of excellent quality or ability
- *"Luigi is a **cracker jack** Italian chef. He has his own TV show."*

them, nor dwell on the fact that he got no change back. Father and son devoured the "dogs" while watching a fiery red sun set over the stadium.

When the game resumed, the Royals took the lead when the Yankee fielders pulled a **boner**. Two outfielders yelled at the same time, "*My ball!*" "*My ball!*" and then collided as they ran to catch it. The batter raced all the way to third base as delirious Royals fans cheered him on. Then the Royals **cleanup** hitter smashed a pitch to right field, and although the ball was caught, the racing base runner slid across home plate just as the catcher tagged him with the ball.

"Safe!" the umpire signaled with his hands. It was **a** very **close call**.

The Yankee coach and players in the **dugout** stormed onto the field to protest the call.

"*Get some glasses, Ump!*" the Yankee fans yelled in support of

---

Boner – n. stupid or clumsy mistake
- "*I made a **boner** today; I dropped the printer cartridge, and the toner spilled all over the floor. What a mess.*"

Cleanup – adj. the fourth hitter in the line-up who is a strong hitter and able to drive home a runner; an effective player
- "*Let's send Paul, our **cleanup** man, to Korea to close the deal. He understands the client, knows the language, and enjoys the culture.*"

A close call – n. a narrow escape from danger or trouble
- "*There was **a close call** today in the sawmill; a huge log fell off the conveyer belt, but fortunately, the employees jumped back and no one was hurt*"

Dugout – n. sunken shelter on either side of the field where opposing team players stay when not on the field

their team, but the umpire wouldn't be persuaded, despite the **rhubarb** between the Yankee manager and the umpire. Finally, the umpire tired of all the arguments and **tossed** the Yankee manager **out of the game.**

Now the Royals led the ballgame, but no one was complacent, for the Yankees were famous for **making a comeback**; they often played their best games when behind.

Suddenly fans all around Jey and Sammy jumped to their feet. A high foul ball sailed toward their seats.

"Catch it, Dad!" Sammy and a dozen other kids screamed at their fathers. Jey's glove was still in his backpack. He reached out bare-handed, but the ball arced just beyond his finger-tips. A dozen hands reached for the ball; two dozen voices shouted, "I got it!"

No one caught the ball. It bounced off plastic seats and along the cement floor while fans tumbled over one another to grab it. Finally the ball dropped into the over-sized glove of a 10-year-old, rosy-cheeked girl in a **ponytail**. She beamed as she cradled her souvenir like she would a doll.

Rhubarb – n. a heated argument, conflict, or disagreement
- "A **rhubarb** broke out between representatives at the trade fair over who would have the booth nearest the door. Security officials were called to control the situation."

Tossed out of the game – v. to be removed from a game or a job because of poor performance; to be ejected for poor sportsmanship
- "John was **tossed out of the game** when the other members of the joint committee could no longer tolerate his incompetence and rudeness."

Make a comeback – v. to achieve a success after retirement or failure
- "The style of jeans everyone thought was outdated has **made a comeback**; all the young people are buying that jeans design again."

Ponytail – n. a hairstyle in which the hair is pulled back from the face and secured, so that it falls like a pony's tail. A ponytail is usually worn by women but sometimes by men.

"**Sign her up**!" several fans cheered. While dozens of fans regretted not getting the ball, no one could begrudge that such a cute kid was going home with a prized memento from a big league ball game.

After this diversion, Jey and Sammy returned their attention to the game. They sat **glued to their seats** as the Royals maintained their one run lead. But then in the top of the ninth inning, the first two Yankee batters got on base with a walk and a base hit. The Royals fans uttered a collective groan as the Yankee runner on second base became the potential tying run, able to score if any of the next three batters should hit even a single to the outfield.

The Kansas City manager called a **time out** and took the tired Royals pitcher out of the game, replacing him with the team's best relief pitcher. Jey clenched his teeth as he focused on the drama between pitcher and batter; he now felt a new appreciation for how exciting baseball could be. Fortunately for the Royals, the Kansas City pitcher struck out the Yankees in order, without a run scoring, allowing the happy Royals fans to stream out of the stadium, pleased to have attended such a thrilling game.

Sign her/him up! – an expression to indicate that a person has done an exceptionally and surprisingly fine job; praise
- *"The visitor to our factory noticed a problem and solved it. Our manager said, '**Sign him up**! We need more creative people like him.'"*

Glued to one's seat – so fascinated or engrossed with ongoing events that one becomes motionless and completely focused on what is happening
- *"The inspirational speech by the new CEO kept all the employees **glued to their seats**."*

Time out – n. a brief cessation of a game, meeting, or process in order to rest, consult, or regroup
- *"The customer posed a technical problem we hadn't addressed, so our team took a one-hour **time out** to explore solutions."*

Eighth Inning

Jey learned shortly after arriving in Missouri that the state's nickname is the "Show Me" state." Missourians are skeptical and not easily impressed, but even they were surprised by the intensity of the early summer's series of storms. Ominous thunderclouds gathered on the eve of many Little League game, so that by game time it was sometimes **raining cats and dogs**. As a result, Sammy's games were often postponed, practice sessions were cancelled, and even the Royals were occasionally forced to hand out **rain checks** to disappointed ticket-holders.

Raining cats and dogs – **adj**. raining very, very hard. This is a strange idiom, not apparently related at all to animals, that was first used in the 17th century. It may refer to such hard rain that dead animals, cats and dogs, were floating in the open sewers of the time.
- *"It **rained cats and dogs** during the company baseball game. The flimsy tents didn't work so everyone left early."*

Rain check – **n**. a ticket stub or receipt or other assurance of admission to a future event if the scheduled event is cancelled due to rain; also, a promise by a store to honor a sale price in the future if the item is sold out; also, a promise that an unaccepted offer will be renewed in the future
- *"Pierre invited me to visit his remodeled art gallery, but I was busy that day, so I asked for a **rain check**."*

Jey was secretly pleased by the sultry summer days of rain. He could remain at his air-conditioned office until well after dark each night without feeling guilty about missing Sammy's games. His project was at a critical stage. He needed to be with his team, **in there pitching** their innovative methodology to an overly-cautious design group who had suddenly **balked** at incorporating Jey's algorithm feature into the proposed product. Jey didn't back down; he insisted the enhancement was necessary.

For the past year, MedicMon had **taken a beating** on the stock market because of its failure to introduce product innovations. Some aggressive competitors were grabbing market share, and the company was **in a slump**. Unless MedicMon introduced a successful

In there pitching – **adv.** actively engaged; trying hard to sell or promote something; working hard.
- *"If we want to win new customers, we've got to be **in there pitching** our expanded product line of organic soups, and offering free soup sampling at the grocery stores we serve."*

Balk – **v.** to refuse, to stop abruptly, to be stubborn; in baseball, an incomplete and illegal motion by the pitcher which results in base runners being allowed to advance one base
- *"The loan officer at the bank wanted to be helpful, but she **balked** when she was asked to approve a high-risk loan."*

Take a beating – **v.** to lose by a wide margin, or to be in an unenviable position; to suffer against something or someone else
- *"The dollar is **taking a beating** against the Euro this year."*

In a slump – **adv.** exhibiting an extended period of poor performance
- *"The auto industry is **in a slump** due to rising oil prices."*

new product to excite the health care industry, the company might find itself forced to sell off its successful product division to a competitor in order to gain working capital to keep the company solvent. The prospect of such a **squeeze play** made every MedicMon employee nervous.

  The bottom line, Jey realized one night as he drove home in pouring rain after struggling with his team to validate the test runs, was that if the project failed, he might as well **hang up his spikes** at MedicMon and search for a new job.

  When he arrived home and walked in the door, even the aroma of Shoba's curry dinner didn't lighten his spirits. Then Sammy came out from his bedroom with a book on baseball in his hands.

Squeeze play – n. pressure exerted to gain a concession or achieve a goal; in baseball, when the batter bunts (hits the ball lightly) to try to advance the third base runner home. The batter expects to be put out at first base, but provides the runner a chance to score. If the batter misses the ball, the base runner is easily put out by the catcher who has the ball from the pitcher in his hand.

- *"The investor tried a **squeeze play**; he bought a large number of shares and tried at the annual stockholder's meeting use his voting shares to force out the company president."*

Hang up one's spikes – v. to retire from baseball, or from a profession

- *"I'm going to **hang up my spikes** after 35 years in the vacuum cleaner business. It's time for my daughter to take over the family operation."*

Baseball shoes with spikes →

"Dad, didn't you say your project at work is called **_Joltin' Joe_**?"

Jey nodded wearily. Each MedicMon project was given an internal code name; Jey was baffled by this name and other names that his colleagues came up with.

"Joltin' Joe was the nickname for Joe DiMaggio," Sammy said, "one of the greatest Yankee baseball players of all time!"

Sammy showed his father the description of Joe DiMaggio in Ken Burns' book, *Baseball*. Jey read that in 1941 Joltin' Joe lifted the spirits of the American people with his 56 game **hitting streak**, a record that has never been broken. The son of Italian immigrants, DiMaggio played center field for the Yankees for 13 years, missing three years to serve in World War II. He played in nine World Series, achieved a life-time batting average of .325, and hit 361 home runs.

"Well, that's interesting," Jey said. He now saw that the code name fit his project. Joltin' Joe DiMaggio shocked his opponents with magnificent hitting and his competitive spirit. Jey reasoned that if his team's complex methodology were successfully adopted by the design team and eventually integrated into products, MedicMon

Joltin' Joe – A nickname for Joe DiMaggio, one of the most famous and talented baseball players of all time. "Joltin" describes how DiMaggio struck the ball hard, knocked the ball over the fence for many home runs, and always gave the fans a "jolt" of excitement. Joe DiMaggio, made his major league debut on May 3, 1936, and he led the New York Yankees to nine championships in 13 years. DiMaggio retired in 1951. He was a legend in his lifetime. Many songs mention him, and many books have been written about him. At the left is Joe DiMaggio's plaque in the Baseball Hall of Fame in Cooperstown, New York.

Hitting streak – n. consecutive number of games in which a player gets a hit; also, to be successful time after time.
- *I'm on a **hitting streak**; I've sold a new car off our lot every day this week."*

would shake up the digital health monitoring industry and give his company a jolt of new revenue and prestige. His company could again be **in the catbird seat**.

Suddenly Jey's spirits soared. His work could really make a difference. Why shouldn't he be the one to lead a series of industry innovations? After all, Joltin Joe DiMaggio had to start his 56 game hitting streak with that first base hit. The important lesson, Jey realized, was to **take a swing at** success.

"Sammy," Jey said after reading the rest of the story about other **Yankee legends**, "notice that the number on Joltin' Joe's uniform is **5**."

In the catbird seat – **adv**. in a position of power or prominence; to be in a superior position. The American catbird consistently seeks out the highest perch in a tree, so he is above all other birds in the same tree. First used widely by an announcer at a baseball game.
- *"Professor Patel is **in the catbird seat**; he was selected to run a major education initiative at the United Nations."*

Take a swing at – **v**. to make an effort, to attempt
- *"I'm not sure I can fix the robotics in that strange new machine, but I'll **take a swing at** it."*

Yankee legends – Beginning with Lou Gehrig's number 4 in 1939, the Yankees have "**retired**" [see definition on page 59] numerous uniform numbers to honor players and managers. Among them are Babe Ruth, Whitey Ford, Joe DiMaggio, Mickey Mantle, Roger Maris, Phil Rizzuto, Casey Stengel and Yogi Berra.

Legend – **n**. a notable person in fields such as art, music, sport, or film who is talked about in his or her lifetime, and is remembered long after he or she has died

54

"That's right!" Sammy smiled, but then his grin suddenly turned into a frown. "But I'll never be a good hitter, Dad."

Jey knew from experience that a **winning attitude** and hard work counted for just as much as talent. Sammy needed a pep talk, just as Shoba's encouraging words often bolstered Jey's spirits when issues at work seemed overwhelming.

"Sammy, my best advice is a phrase we use all the time at work: **touch all your bases**. Focus on the fundamentals, practice every day, and just keep swinging that bat."

Jey was pleased that his son listened, not because Jey was an expert on baseball, but because touching all the bases was fundamental to success. Jey admitted to himself that he should apply his own advice at work. He needed to touch base with other researchers, contact his Japanese partner to lay the groundwork for the upcoming face-to-face meeting, and **have the book on** the internal design engineers so he could influence them to include his features in MedicMon products.

"Dad, you're daydreaming again." Sammy took the book out his father's hands.

Shoba entered the dining room. "Make sure to mark your calendar for two weeks from Friday," she said as she motioned him

---

Winning attitude – n. a confident outlook; a belief in oneself and in success
- "Sue has a ***winning attitude***, which has helped her rise to Senior Vice President."

Touch all one's [the] bases – v. to perform all the steps necessary to further one's goal. In baseball, a runner must touch all the bases as he runs around the diamond if he is to score a run.
- "Our mayor **touched all the bases** before re-organizing the city departments, since so many employees and contractors were affected."

Have the book on - v. to be informed about or have knowledge and history about a person or situation that will be advantageous
- "Before negotiating the deal, we **had the book on** everyone who was sitting across the table from us."

to the table, where one of his favorite meals awaited him. "That's the last game of Sammy's season, since some of the postponed games can't be **made up**."

"And I'm going to get the game-winning hit," Sammy said with confidence as he slid into his chair and reached for the bowl of rice.

Suddenly Jey didn't feel hungry. On that very day he was scheduled to be in Tokyo for the critical meeting with his Japanese partner. How would he **break the news to** his son and wife that he would be a **no-show** at Sammy's final game?

Make up - v. to re-schedule or substitute for a cancellation or missed opportunity
- *"Jose **made up** all the classes that he missed when he was ill."*

Break the news – v. to tell someone unwelcome or unpleasant information
- *"I hate to **break the news** to you, but your job is being eliminated."*

No-show – n. someone who doesn't appear for an important engagement
- *"My dentist sends me a bill if I'm a **no-show** for my dental appointment."*

Top of the Ninth Inning

After Sammy went to bed that evening, Shoba sat at the dining room table and listened as Jey explained his dilemma. She agreed that he had a hard call to make, but she expected him to be at Sammy's last game.

The next morning and each morning thereafter, Jey woke before dawn, aware that **the clock was ticking** and he had just a few days to decide whether to fly to Tokyo with his colleagues to attend the important meeting with MedicMon's partner, or send a pinch hitter.

By the end of the week, when Jey couldn't make a decision, he booked a conference room for his team, asked Dave to call in from home, and told them of his conflict. Karl and Dave both had sons who played Little League, and Yoko's daughter was the star pitcher of a girl's team, so they all commiserated with him. Yet they agreed that Jey was the technical expert and therefore should be the **designated hitter** for MedicMon's crucial presentation in Tokyo.

The clock is ticking – a phrase meaning that time is running out; the lack of time has become a pressure
- *"**The clock is ticking**; if we don't get our proposal in by 5 pm today, we'll lose an opportunity to be on the short list for the highway paving contract."*

Designated hitter – n. in baseball, a player who enters the game only to hit for the pitcher; a strong performer who is likely to succeed
- *"Tina, you're our **designated hitter** for the presentation; it's up to you to convince the investor to provide another round of working capital."*

An hour later, they left the conference room with a plan for solving Jey's dilemma. The plan would require team effort, technology, and precise timing, not to mention some luck.

Jey walked to his cubicle, where he would **hole up** for the coming days as he completed his patent disclosure, networked with colleagues throughout the industry, and collaborated with his team on the Tokyo presentation. He felt the heavy weight of an enormous **Louisville slugger** on his shoulder. If he struck out, he, his team, and even his company risked being reduced to **minor-league** status in the industry.

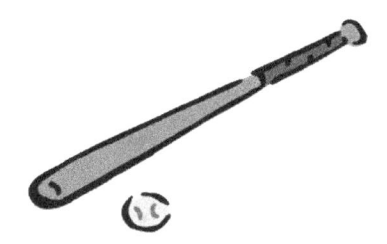

Sammy missed sharing the weekend batting practice with his father, but he benefited from daily team practice, now that the weather had again turned sunny. He knew nothing of his father's hard choice; his mind was focused on hitting the ball the way Joltin' Joe DiMaggio did — in the clutch to win the game.

Hole up – v. to spend time alone; to be unavailable to others, usually in order to concentrate on work or a special project
- *"Angie **holed up** in a rural family cabin so that she could finish her novel."*

Louisville slugger – n. a baseball bat, named after the company that first made the bats in 1884 in Louisville, Kentucky

Minor-league – n. sports leagues that are regarded as less than premier; not the top league
- *"To move up from the **minor leagues** in our industry, we need to increase our market share and gain brand recognition in Europe and Asia."*

Often during practice sessions Sammy **got a piece of** the ball, but he rarely got a base hit; usually the balls sailed or rolled **out of bounds**. Still, Sammy kept in mind the stories of the great baseball stars he read about at night in his room, including Jackie Robinson, the first African-American to play in the major leagues. Among the Yankee players, Lou Gehrig, Mickey Mantle and Babe Ruth were his favorites. For the Royals, George Brett, whose number, like Joltin' Joe's, had **been retired**, was one of Sammy's heroes. Sammy got inspiration from reading about their struggles to become stars.

During the last practice day before the big game between the *Bears* and their cross-city rival, the *Eagles,* Sammy spied his father at the ballpark. He waved, but his Dad seemed absorbed in surveying a nearby power pole and trees, the shuttered concession trailer, the bleachers and the school building across the parking lot behind the home plate fence.

On Friday afternoon, a cloudless sky greeted *Bears* and *Eagles* players and fans as they filled the bleachers. The boys **warmed up** on the field an hour before game time. Shoba took her customary seat in the bleachers, a spot where she could see Sammy both when he was at bat and when he stood in centerfield.

Everyone stood for the National Anthem played on an iPod hooked up to powerful speakers. Then the *Bears*, who enjoyed the

---

A piece of – n. in baseball, contact with the ball but not a solid hit; a portion of what is desired, but not all [may be a positive or negative outcome]
- *"We're thrilled our firm got **a piece of** the military hardware contract."*

Out of bounds – adj. beyond the designated boundaries or limits
- *"Wearing swimwear to work is completely **out of bounds**."*

Retired – v. (passive) no longer used, as a player's number, or a product
- *"Because of the rapidly changing demographics, our best-selling product last year will soon **be retired**. We need to appeal to a younger consumer."*

Warm up – v. to practice, to loosen up [oneself or others] in preparation for the main event; in baseball, pitchers and players warm up before the game starts
- *"Before going into the main points of my presentation, I'm going to **warm up** the audience with a personal story."*

home team advantage, raced onto the field.

Sammy took his position in centerfield and searched the bleachers for his father. A frown crossed his face; how could his father be late again?

"**Heads up**, boys!" the *Bears* coach yelled to the fielders, and the game got underway with an *Eagles* base hit that Sammy fielded quickly and threw back to the infield. The *Eagles* managed to score two runs in that first inning; the *Bears* answered with two runs in their half of the inning.

In the second inning when Sammy stood at the plate ready to bat for the first time, he glanced toward the bleachers. There was his father, perched on the top row of the bleachers. He wore headphones attached to an open laptop. Next to him sat Yoko, his father's work colleague. She pointed a digital camera at him while also talking into a headset.

"Play ball," the umpire urged Sammy.

Sammy stepped into the batters box and tried to concentrate. All the advice he'd read and heard from his coach swirled in his head: *"Watch the ball. Swing smoothly. Follow through. Step into the ball. Don't swing too hard."*

The pitcher, a **southpaw**, hadn't yet **settled down**, and he

---

Home team advantage – n. favorable conditions enjoyed by teams playing in a familiar location where their fans are present and cheering them on
- *"In the upcoming trade talks, we've got the **home team advantage**. We're in our own city and negotiating in our native language."*

Heads up – v. to make others alert to potential danger or trouble
- *"**Heads up,** everyone. Make sure all the kitchen appliances and counters are clean; the government food inspector is visiting our restaurant this morning."*

Southpaw – n. a pitcher who throws left-handed; anyone who is left-handed
- *"As a **southpaw**, I prefer a different mouse for my computer."*

Settle down – v. to become calm, measured, more rational, less agitated
- *"Once the stock market **settles down**, I'm going to invest more money."*
- *"Just **settle down**. The airline will find your lost luggage."*

threw several balls into the dirt. Sammy **drew a walk**.

"*Good eye*," a parent shouted approval as Sammy ran down to first base. When Sammy looked up, he saw the camera pointed at him on first base. When his teammate hit a long fly ball that the *Eagles* outfielder bobbled, Sammy scooted around the bases and crossed the plate. He grinned from ear to ear; his quick base-running had put his team ahead. As he plopped down in the dugout and gulped a cup of water, his friends asked him what his father was doing up in the bleachers. Sammy shrugged. He had stopped trying to figure out his father's odd behavior.

Draw a walk – v. to be patient when batting; to refrain from swinging at poor pitches, so that when the pitcher throws four pitches which the umpire judges are outside the strike zone, the batter is entitled to "walk" to first base

Bottom of the Ninth Inning

Jey kept one eye on the game, the other on his laptop with the mounted camera and the WiFi technology that he was using to connect to the Tokyo conference site. An hour earlier, Jey had emailed his presentation slides to the conference room, and now he was streaming his voice with his photo so that he could present his methodology "live," as well as view the Japanese participants via their high-tech video system.

The seemingly **screwball** idea for the videoconferencing meeting from the schoolyard bleachers came from Yoko. When she explained to the Japanese why Jey would find it difficult to be at the meeting, they asked about Sammy and his team. Jey learned from Yoko that the Japanese were avid baseball fans. Their superstar was **Ichiro Suzuki**, who played for the Seattle Mariners. Yoko suggested that

---

Screwball – **adj**. a pitched ball that curves in the opposite direction of a normal curve ball; thus, odd, eccentric, crazy
- *"That's a **screwball** idea for a new product; no one will seriously consider it."*

Ichiro Suzuki – Ichiro Suzuki (鈴木一朗) is the right fielder for the Seattle Mariners. He became the first Japanese-born everyday position player in the Major Leagues. In 2004 Suzuki set a new all-time, single-season Major League record with 262 hits.

Jey attend the meeting by videoconference, and also send **play-by-play** updates of the game to Tokyo during breaks in the meeting.

Jey was at first dubious, but Yoko assured him the meeting could be a win-win: business mixed with baseball, one of Japan's passions. Yoko asked the Japanese staff to come in 30 minutes earlier than usual. A 5 p.m. game time in Kansas City meant that it would start at 9 a.m. in Japan. So on the day of the game the Tokyo staff arrived at 8:30 to set everything up, enabling them to start the meeting promptly at 9.

In order to ensure that the meeting would run smoothly, Jey had touched base with numerous people the previous week. He set up an extension cord from his laptop to an electrical outlet on the popcorn and drinks trailer at the ball field, and he tested the school's high-speed Internet access to make sure his laptop would pick up a strong signal. Yoko double-checked the audio and tried out several zoom lenses.

When Sammy's game started, Jey connected to the video conference with his Japanese colleagues. After he joked about his bandaged nose and showed a clip of the ballpark, he began the presentation of his advanced methodology.

Meanwhile Yoko took video clips of the game to be transmitted to Japan and shown there during breaks in Jey's presentation. Yoko reported to Jey that the showing of the game's **highlights** resulted in considerable interest and lively discussions in Tokyo.

Play-by-play – n. an ongoing account of each play during the game, given by a radio or TV announcer
- *"Give me a **play-by-play** of the meeting. What did each person say about the technical choices that were being debated?"*

Highlights – n. especially interesting or significant events
- *"The TV commentator touched on the **highlights** of the President's speech to the nation."*

Both the Tokyo meeting and the baseball game progressed smoothly, until the bottom of the ninth inning. The game was tied, 7 to 7, the *Bears* had players in scoring position, and the excited crowd of competing Little League parents yelled so loudly that Jey couldn't hear much on his headset. The Tokyo people asked what was happening. Jey yelled that Sammy was at bat. He wanted to remain calm enough to continue his presentation, but his hands were shaking, as he sat on the edge of his seat.

At the plate, Sammy rested his bat on his shoulder while he adjusted his batting helmet. If he felt the tension, and heard the shouting and the encouraging words from his mother and other parents, he didn't show it. Yoko spoke quickly in Japanese into her headset. "I've suggested another tea break," she translated for Jey.

"Thanks. I'm so nervous I can't even speak."

Sammy was mumbling to himself. No one, however, would have guessed that Sammy was whispering, "*Joltin' Joe, Joltin Joe,*" as if to give himself courage.

Sammy swung and missed the first pitch. Groans came from the *Bears* side of the bleachers. The next three pitches were out of the strike zone. Sammy hit two foul balls into the bleachers, to make it a **full count**. Shoba, Jey and everyone became silent, as if holding in a collective breath.

Full count – n. the batter has three balls and two strikes, so he will either get on base or be put out; a deciding moment
- "It's ***a full count***, *folks. We need to decide whether to close down the outdated facility and go into debt to build a new manufacturing line, or else stick with the old line and hope the machines don't break down.*"

Then an encouraging voice from the bleachers shattered the silence. "**It ain't over till it's over!** Win it for us, Sammy!"

The pitcher delivered the next pitch.

Crack!

The ball soared into right field. Back, back the *Eagles* fielder raced, but the ball sailed over his head and rolled to the fence. The base runners scored. The *Bears* won! Sammy's teammates raced onto the field to encircle Sammy and give each other **high fives**.

Jey jumped up. "Sammy won the game!" Jey shouted into the headset. "Sammy won the game! He got the clutch hit!"

"Where are the pictures?" the team in Tokyo asked excitedly from half a world away, even as they clapped. "Pictures, please," they asked.

"Yoko is sending you the video. It's coming through soon." Yoko scrambled to put it all together as Jey descended the bleacher steps. Suddenly he got a **charley horse**. He winced as he limped over to Shoba, who was shedding tears of joy.

"It ain't over til it's over" – Famous statement from Yankee catcher and manager, Yogi Berra, meaning that there's always hope of winning until the last out occurs. Yogi Berra's memorable statements are often quoted. For other quotes by Yogi Berra, go to: www.yogiberra.com

High five – n. a gesture of elation or victory in which the upturned palm of one person slaps the palm of another person

Charley horse – n. a cramp or stiffness in a muscle, especially of the upper leg. The origin of this term from baseball is unknown.

"Our son," Shoba grinned, and held Jey's hand. Then she wiped her eyes, and looked up. "Why are you wearing those headphones?" she asked. "And limping? And what is Yoko doing?"

"I'll tell you everything later," Jey said. For those glorious few moments, he wanted nothing to distract him from watching his son enjoy the feeling of success.

As joyful and disappointed parents and boys slowly moved to the parking lot to drive to the pizza hall for the end of the season party, Sammy ran up to his parents.

"Mom, Dad, I'm going to be a baseball player when I grow up!"

Shoba and Jey smiled at one another. "Well," said Shoba, "You might have more fun playing baseball than being a mathematician like your father."

"Oh, I had fun today," Jey winked. "And **just wait til next year**." Then he hobbled back up the bleacher steps to resume his meeting.

Wait [un]til next year – a statement often said by those who are looking to the future for a new season or a new start
- *"We broke even this first year on our drive-thru coffee shop, but just **wait til next year** when that new office complex across the street is finished. We'll make a profit"*

Please request your <u>free</u> download of the audio reading of the story, *Touch All the Bases*.

**Simply write to:
downloads@jolindaosborne.com**

Put this word in the subject line.

| fastball |

You will receive a reply with easy instructions on how to download the MP3 audio of the story.

Baseball Fundamentals

The baseball season in America stretches from **Spring Training** exhibition games in early March, through the lazy days of summer, and into October, when the **World Series** Championship series is played by the best teams in the American and National Leagues.

Major League professional games are broadcast by TV networks, and the results are prominently reported in newspaper and internet sports pages. However, semi-professional, amateur, and Little League teams abound. On any summer day or evening, fans can watch a neighborhood ballgame, or participate on local teams.

Following is a brief overview of baseball rules, plays and equipment.

The game is played by two opposing teams of nine players, each team alternating in the **field** and **at bat**. The **home team** bats last. In order to score a point, called a **run**, a batter must move around a course of three canvas bag **bases** laid out in a diamond pattern and return **home**, the fourth base made out of a rubber plate.

Home plate   **One of the Three Bases**

Batters use **bats** made from the wood of the ash tree to try to hit a leather-covered, hard **baseball**. Batters may also use metal bats.

In the field, called a **diamond**, there are a pitcher, catcher, four infielders and three outfielders. The pitcher initiates each play by throwing a variety of **pitches** [**fastball**, **screwball**, **curve ball**] from the pitcher's mound to **home plate**. An opposing team's batter attempts to hit the pitches and safely reach base, while the fielders attempt to put the batter out, by catching a hit ball or tagging the batter before he reaches a base.

A batter who misses three pitches or fails to swing at three pitches in the **strike zone,** roughly between the armpits and knees, is out on **strikes**. If the pitcher throws four pitches out of the strike zone, the batter obtains a **walk** and advances to first base. A **run** is scored every time a batter becomes a runner and crosses home plate after touching each base in the prescribed order.

A batter may hit a **fair ball**, which is played, or a **foul** ball which is **out of bounds** of the playing field and is replayed. If a ball is hit over the fence, it becomes a **home run** and the batter and all other runners on base will score. A mistake made by a fielder or runner is an **error**.

Umpires ensure that players follow the rules. In this illustration, an umpire is seen calling a player out, either because he has three strikes or because he has been tagged out by an opposing player. When the fielding team puts out three batters or runners, half of an **inning** has been played and the teams exchange places. The team with more runs at the end of **nine innings** [or after extra innings if there is a tie] wins the game. Unlike other sports with set time limits, baseball has no time clock. Normally a game takes about three hours, but games continue for as long as it takes a team to win — one of the longest major league game was played for over 8 hours!

A season consists of many games, so even though a team loses some games, it might still be ranked the top team for the season. Professional baseball also has special games, such as an **All-Star Game**, when the best players from all the teams exhibit their skills for the fans.

Great baseball players can be voted by sports writers into the **Baseball Hall of Fame**, located in Cooperstown, New York. The baseball museum in Cooperstown is visited annually by millions of baseball fans. Over the years, baseball stars have had their pictures and career statistics printed on baseball cards, which fans collect. Some very old cards are quite valuable.

Resources for Continued Learning

Classic Films/Videos that depict American Baseball
- *Baseball: A Nine-part PBS Home Video Documentary*
- *Bull Durham*
- *The Natural*
- *Damn Yankees*

Books about Baseball: There are literally hundreds of books about baseball!
- *Baseball: An Illustrated History*, Geoffrey Ward
- *Promises to Keep: How Jackie Robinson Changed Baseball,* Sharon Robinson
- *Once More Around the Park,* Roger Angell

Venues for Watching Baseball
- *Network, cable, and satellite TV all cover professional sports*
- *Attend a city, Little League, high school, or college baseball game*
- *When in a major league town, view a professional ball game*

Internet Sites:
- *Major League Baseball www.mlb.com*
- *Legendary players: www.jackierobinson.com; www.joedimaggio.com*

Dictionaries
- *Dictionary.com*
- *Random House Webster's Unabridged Dictionary* [book or CD Rom that enables you to listen to the pronunciation of words]
- *Newberry House Dictionary.* The book uses the International Phonetic Alphabet; the CD Rom enables you to listen to pronunciation of words.

Other books and products to help you master American English
- If you have difficulty pronouncing American English, these educational products will help you:
    - *American Accent for Success in Business: A Complete Video CD-ROM Course*
    - *Improve your Spoken English and Pronunciation: An American Accent Course for Success in Business,* with downloadable MP3 audio
- Other books in the series: Stories for Learning Useful Business Idioms
    - *Against All Odds: The Culture and Idioms of Risk-taking in America*
    - *Take the Bull by the Horns: The Culture and Idioms of the American Wild West*

Read about these other books and products at: www.jolindaosborne.com

Index of Idioms

A numbers game - n. slang for a way of looking at betting, games or life by figuring out the odds   43

A piece of - n. in baseball, contact with the ball but not a solid hit; a portion of what is desired, but not all [may be a positive or negative outcome]   59

Add insult to injury - v. to hurt a person's feelings after doing him harm; to make a bad situation worse   14

American pastime - n. a term used to describe baseball. Baseball is one of the oldest organized sports. Baseball games are played in nearly all American cities (and in many countries around the world) at the professional, semi-professional, amateur and Little League levels. A pastime is a way of spending recreational or spare time in a pleasant manner.   16

At bat - adv. in a position to make something happen   13

At the top of one's game - adv. at the height of one's ability or achievement   35

Balk - n. v. in baseball, an incomplete and illegal motion by the pitcher which allows base runners to advance one base; to refuse, to stop abruptly, to be stubborn.   51

Ballpark estimate/figure - n. a guess, an estimate   41

Baseball card - n. cards, usually 2 ½ x 3 ½ inches, with a color photo of a baseball player on one side, and statistics about that player on the other side   16

Batter - n. player whose turn it is to stand at the plate and try to hit the ball   11

Batting average - n. performance of hitters obtained by dividing the number of hits by the total number of times at bat; a performance measurement   42

Batting helmet - n. protective headgear worn by a batter to prevent injury from a pitched ball   14

Be up - v. in baseball, to be the batter waiting to come to the plate to try to hit the ball; to be the next in line to take action   31

Bean - v. to hit the batter on the head with a pitched baseball   21

Bench - n. v. reserve players on a team [who sit on a bench and wait]; to take someone out of the game or out of the action   18

Better late than never - an expression said in exasperation at a delay   10

Bleachers - n. a tiered stand of wooden or metal seats and steps   10

Boner - n. a stupid or clumsy mistake   47

Break the news - v. to tell someone difficult or unpleasant information   56

Bronx cheer - n. a loud sound made with the lips and tongue that expresses disapproval, usually in response to players or umpires at a game   40

Bum - n. an incompetent, lazy, useless person. At times, baseball fans call their team members bums when they don't perform as expected.   45

Bush-league - adj. not of a professional standard; inadequate or unsophisticated, as if coming from the undeveloped countryside (the bushes)   45

Cap - n. a baseball player's brimmed hat, usually sporting a team logo   11

Catch - v. to understand something, usually quickly or in small parts   40

Caught napping - v. [passive] have failed to respond because of inattention   12

Chalk something up to experience - v. to learn from one's mistake and move forward with better understanding   41

Charley horse - n. a cramp or stiffness in a muscle, especially of the upper leg. The origin of this term first used in baseball is unknown.   65
Cheer on - v. to encourage   39
Choke - v. to fail to perform effectively because of nervousness or tension   44
Clean out - v. to empty of contents; leave bare   23
Clock is ticking - a phrase meaning that time is running out; the lack of time has become a pressure   57
Cleanup - adj. description of the fourth hitter in the line-up who is a strong hitter and able to drive home any runners already on base; effective in getting the job done   47
Close call - n. a narrow escape from danger or trouble   47
Clout - n. power, strength or influence; in baseball, a hard hit   20
Clutch hitter - n. a player who gets a hit when runners are in scoring position; a person to be relied on to make an enterprise successful   15
Come out of left field - v. to appear unexpectedly and without warning   20
Come up with - v. to devise, create, think up   25
Coolers - n. insulated containers, often taken to ball games or picnics, for keeping food and drinks cold   34
Cracker Jack™ - n. a trademarked brand of caramel-coated popcorn with peanuts, sold in small boxes with a prize inside; idiomatically, the term means of excellent quality or ability   46
Cricket - n. a sport popular in British Commonwealth countries, played with balls and bats by teams of 11 players. Good sportsmanship and adherence to proper etiquette are stressed. Something **not cricket** is unfair.   11
Designated hitter - n. a player who enters the game only to hit for the pitcher; a strong batter who is likely to perform well   57
Diamond - n. the field upon which baseball is played, so called because of the shape of the infield with its four bases   23
Draw a walk - v. to be patient when batting and refrain from swinging at poor pitches, so that when the pitcher throws four pitches which the umpire judges are outside the strike zone, the batter is entitled to "walk" to first base   61
Dugout - n. the sunken shelters on the sidelines of the diamond where players stay when not on the field   47
Error - n. a mistake made by a fielder   12
Fair ball - n. a ball that is in play, meaning that the runners may advance and the fielders can try to make an out   44
Fan - n. an ardent devotee, an enthusiast   39
Farm out - v. to assign something to an outsider or contractor. Baseball teams often have farm teams where they send potentially excellent young players to gain experience and confidence.   18
Fast out of the box - adj. describes a good start, [as a hitter running to first base]; thus, a quick learner   18
Fastball - n. a pitch thrown at up to 100 miles per hour in the hope that the batter will not be able to hit it   30
Field - v. in baseball, to retrieve the baseball after it has been hit by the batter; in business, to respond to difficult questions from an audience   21
Friendly confines - n. a term for the home team's baseball stadium   27

Full count - n. the batter has three balls and two strikes, so he will either get on base or be put out; a deciding moment   64
Fundamentals - n. (The) whatever is essential or necessary   26, 68
Game of inches - n. game or situation in which the slightest variation is important; an arena or field of work where accuracy is critical   44
Game plan - n. a strategy; a method of execution   20
Get to first base - v. to achieve the first step; to succeed in an initial phase   15
Give one hundred and ten percent - v. to exert more effort and energy than is expected, but which may be necessary for success   29
Glove - n. equipment specially designed for fielding and catching a baseball   10
Glued to one's seat - so fascinated with ongoing events that one becomes motionless or completely focused on what is happening   49
Go to bat for - v. actively support or help   20
Good in the clutch - adj. able to make the important play under pressure or in a critical situation   32
Goose egg - n. zero, especially when written numerically   15
Hang loose - v. slang for "take it easy" or relax   42
Hang up one's spikes - v. to retire from baseball, or to retire from any profession   52
Have legs - adj. ability to survive or thrive; good enough to succeed   19
Have no one in the bullpen - phrase meaning to be without help. In baseball, a relief pitcher comes in from the bullpen when the current pitcher has trouble getting batters out, but if no pitchers are left in the bullpen, the team will not win.   19
Have something on the ball - adj. especially capable, efficient or talented; in baseball, description of a pitcher who throws a type of pitched ball that hitters can't hit   32
Have the book on - v. to be informed about or have knowledge and history about a person or situation that will be advantageous   55
Have to admit - v. to acknowledge that something is true, despite one's reluctance to do so   25
Hawker - n. one who sells something aggressively by yelling or calling out   41
Head south - v. to go in the wrong direction, to go off course   17
Heads up - v. call to others to be alert; to watch out for potential danger   60
High five - n. a gesture of elation or victory in which the upturned palm of one person slaps the palm of another person   65
Highlights - n. interesting or significant events; summation   63
Hitting streak - n. consecutive number of games in which a player gets a hit; also, a series of successes   53
Hole up - v. to spend time alone; to be unavailable to others, usually in order to concentrate on work   58
Home Run - n. a big accomplishment or success   14
Home team advantage - n. favorable conditions enjoyed by teams playing in familiar surroundings with the team's fans looking on   59
Hot dog - n. a sausage made of pork, beef, chicken or, in certain modern ballparks, tofu, and served in a long, soft bun. Ballparks are noted for their hot dogs; used idiomatically, a person who shows off   36
Ice down - v. to put ice on an injury in order to reduce swelling   34

Ichiro Suzuki - Ichiro Suzuki (鈴木一朗) is the right fielder for the Seattle Mariners. He became the first Japanese-born everyday position player in the Major Leagues. 62
In a slump - adv. exhibiting an extended period of poor performance   51
In scoring position - adv. within reach of success; in baseball, runners are positioned on 2nd or 3rd base   31
In seventh heaven - adv. in a state of great joy and satisfaction   27
In shape - adj. physically fit; in a state of readiness or good condition   27
In the catbird seat - adv. in a superior position of power or prominence   54
In there pitching - adv. actively engaged; trying hard to sell or promote something; working hard   51
In tow - adv. in one's charge   28
Inning - n. in baseball, one of 9 periods in the game in which each team has the opportunity to score "runs" before making three "outs;" in business, a window of opportunity to act or speak out; a time-limited chance for accomplishment   9
Instant replay - n. video of a sports play that is played back so viewers in the bleachers or at home in front of their TVs can see the play again and/or analyze the play   17
It ain't over til it's over - famous statement from Yankee catcher and manager, Yogi Berra, meaning that until the last out occurs there's always hope of winning 65
It's not whether you win or lose but how you play the game - often-cited advice that emphasizes effort and sportsmanship over winning   35
Joltin' Joe - a nickname for Joe DiMaggio, one of the best baseball players of all time; 'Joltin' describes how he struck the ball hard and made many base hits. He is most famously known for his 56 game hitting streak. 53
Kansas City Royals - The Kansas City Royals are in the Central Division of the American League. George Brett, a three-time AL batting champion, is one of the most famous players to have played for the Royals. 38
Keep one's eye on the ball - v. to remain alert, attentive and focused; good advice for a player of any sport that uses a ball   26
Knock one out of the box - v. to hit the ball hard for a home run; be successful   34
La-Z-Boy ™ **- n.** popular brand of padded, recliner chairs often placed in front of the TV. Many different brands of this type of chair exist, but the name La-Z-Boy has become synonymous with a comfortable spot to view a baseball or other sports game.   27
Legend - n. a notable person in fields such as art, music, sport, or film who is talked about in his or her lifetime, and is remembered long after he or she has died   54
Like never before - adv. more or better than what has previously existed   19
Lineup - n. in baseball or other sports, players who are in the game; people who are part of a team; in business, a selection of products   22
Little League - n. a non-profit US-based organization which organizes local children's leagues of baseball and softball throughout the US, as well as around the world   10
Look over someone's shoulders - v. to scrutinize, pay close attention, often in a suspicious way; to micro-manage   43
Loosen up - v. to relax the muscles; slang similar to **take it easy**   33
Louisville slugger - n. a baseball bat, so named after the company that first made the bats in 1884 in Louisville, Kentucky   58

Major League - adj. describing the best professional players or teams in any sport, as opposed to the minor league players and teams who are usually young and unproven; thus, important or significant   23
Make a comeback - v. to achieve a success after retirement or failure   48
Make a grandstand play - v. to show off or act ostentatiously; first used in baseball to describe a play made to look more difficult than it really is in order to win applause from the fans in the grandstand   40
Make or break - v. to result in great success or complete failure   25
Make the hard call - v. to make a difficult, often emotional decision   29
Make up - v. to re-schedule or substitute for a cancellation or missed opportunity   56
Meal ticket - n. a source of financial support   30
Minor-league - adj. sports leagues that are regarded as less than premier; not the top league   58
Miss by a country mile - v. to miss by a very large margin; to make an obvious mistake or misjudgment   33
Moxie - n. courage, pluck, perseverance, showing confidence   18
National Anthem - n. The Star-Spangled Banner is the national anthem of the United States. It is always sung before the start of a baseball game as well as before the start of many other sporting events.   40
New York Yankees - Arguably, the most famous and successful Major League baseball team, having won 27 World Series Championships   23
No runs, no hits, no errors - the summary of a half inning of play in which nothing of significance occurred in the baseball game; nothing to report   31
No-show - n. a person who fails to appear for an appointment   56
Off-base - adj. in baseball, not on the base, so liable to be called out; not correct, not legal, not workable, not aligned properly   22
Off one's game - adj. not working or functioning at one's best; not in top form   44
Official Program - n. a magazine-style program provided at the sports stadium for attendees; includes information about both teams that are playing that day and the statistics on each player's performance   39
On base - adv. in baseball, to be in a safe position   13
On deck - adv. scheduled to bat next; available, ready to take action   13
On the fly - adv. catching the ball in flight; in a hurry, or on the run   11
Out of bounds - adj. beyond the designated boundaries or limits   59
Out of one's league - adj. beyond one's area of expertise or ability   17
Pep talk - n. a short speech designed to boost enthusiasm or improve morale   15
Pinch hit - v. to substitute one batter for another, usually a better hitter for a weaker one; to take over under pressure   19
Pitcher - n. the **pitcher** throws to the batter to start play in baseball; to **pitch** is to toss something; in business, to attempt to promote or sell   13
Play hardball - v. to act aggressively, ruthlessly or unethically   18
Play-by-play - n. an on-going account of each play and occurrence during a game, given by a radio or TV announcer, or today by a blogger   63
Ponytail - n. hairstyle in which the hair is pulled back from the face and secured so that it falls like a pony's tail; a style usually worn by women but also by some men   48
Pro - n. short for professional, a person recognized for his or her skills   38

Rain check - n. a ticket stub, receipt, or other assurance of admission to a future event if the scheduled event is cancelled due to rain or other reasons   50
Raining cats and dogs - adj. raining very, very hard. This is a strange idiom, not apparently related at all to animals, that was first used in the 17th century.   50
Razz - v. to deride, heckle, tease, make fun of   12
Retired - v. [passive] removed from activity or use, as a famous player's number or an old product   59
Rhubarb - n. a heated argument, conflict, or disagreement   48
Right off the bat - adv. immediately, instantly   38
Roll one's eyes - v. to signal disbelief, astonishment, or mild disapproval by moving the eyes in a circle   40
Rookie - n. an untrained or inexperienced person; a new hire; in baseball, a first year professional player   30
Scoreboard - n. a large board near the outfield fence that shows the hits, runs, and errors for both sides; a means of tracking progress   9
Screwball - adj. a pitched ball that curves in the opposite direction of a normal curve ball; thus, odd, eccentric, crazy   62
Send someone to the showers - v. to remove from the game or from the action   28
Send someone down to the minors - v. to demote, punish, or reduce someone's responsibilities. [The Minor League isn't as important as the Major League in baseball or other sports.]   35
Settle down - v. become calm, more rational, less agitated   60
Seventh Inning Stretch - n. a juncture after six and a half innings of play when fans stand and stretch their legs, get snacks, and sing baseball's famous 1927 song, *Take me Out to the Ball Game*; any break in the action   46
Show a talent for - v. to exhibit innate ability, talent or potential   43
Sign her/him up! – An expression to indicate that the person has done an exceptionally and surprisingly fine job; praise   49
Southpaw - n. a pitcher who throws left-handed; anyone who is left-handed   60
Sponsor - n. a person or organization that provides financial support   11
Sporting - v. [to sport] to wear something in the hope that others will notice   37
Sports page - n. section in the newspaper or online with all the sports news   38
Sportsmanship - n. conduct and attitude when playing sports: fair play, courtesy, grace when losing   33
Squeeze play - n. pressure exerted to gain a concession or achieve a goal; in baseball when the batter bunts to try to advance the third-base runner home   52
Stands - n. bleachers at a playing field or stadium   34
Stats - n. short for statistics; in baseball, various measurements of a ball player's performance   42
Step up to the plate - v. in baseball, to aggressively stand at home plate and prepare to hit the pitched ball; in life, to face a challenge   9
Stranded - v. [passive] to be left on base and unable to score a run; to be left without help or rescue   35
Strike out - v. to fail to hit the ball when standing at the plate; thus, to fail in an endeavor or in an effort   13

Strike Three! - n. the call by the umpire that the batter has lost his last chance to get a hit and must sit down; an admission of failure   14
Strike zone - n. the area over home plate where a pitch must be thrown to be called a stroke, roughly between the armpits and knees; a targeted area to measure success   21
Sweet spot - n. the place on the bat where it is most effective to hit the ball; anything with the optimum characteristics for success   25
Take a bad bounce - v. when a baseball bounces in a way that is unexpected, it might lead to an error; thus, to lead to a miscalculation or unwelcome outcome   44
Take a beating - v. to lose by a wide margin; to be penalized; to be in an unenviable position   51
Take a breather - v. to take a break or to relax   42
Take a swing at - v. to make an effort or an attempt   54
Take the lead - v. to be ahead in a game; to take leadership of something   12
Tale - n. an entertaining story, often with a mix of truth and exaggeration   37
Throw a curve - v. to surprise, fool, or outmaneuver someone   22
Time out - n. a brief cessation of a game or a procedure in order to rest, discuss strategy, or consult with others 49
Toss around - v. to toss a ball around from one player to another; idiomatically, to discuss or debate an issue 13
Tossed out of the game - v. to be removed from a game or a job because of poor performance, or to be ejected for poor sportsmanship   48
Touch all one's [the] bases - v. to perform all the necessary details to further one's goal: contact people, do research, keep everyone informed, etc. In baseball, a runner must touch all the bases if he is to score a run.   55
Touch base with - v. to renew contact or communicate with; in baseball, a runner must touch the bases in order while advancing around the diamond   30
Tug of war - n. a contest of strength in which two teams pull on ends of a rope and try to pull the other team across a dividing line; a struggle for supremacy   22
Two down, one to go - a statement in baseball that two of three outs have been completed; almost complete   31
Two strikes against [someone] - adj. in a precarious or unenviable situation; in danger; about to lose   14
Wait [un]til next year - a statement often said by those who have lost, but are hopeful of a new season or a new start; a look to the future   66
Walk - n. v.   If the pitcher throws four pitches that the umpire judges are outside the strike zone, he has allowed "a walk" and the batter is entitled to "walk" to first base.   15
Warm up - v. to practice, to loosen up [oneself or others] in preparation for the main event   59
Wheaties Breakfast of Champions™ - n. a popular American breakfast cereal of flaked wheat that is eaten with milk. Wheaties is a trademark protected brand from General Mills Company, and was first produced in 1924.   22
Winning attitude - n. a confident attitude, a belief in oneself and in success   55
With the best of them - adv. as well as anyone else   12

Notes

Made in United States
Orlando, FL
11 August 2023